You Sold What to Whom?

by
Ken Carpenter

authorHOUSE®

AuthorHouse™
1663 Liberty Drive, Suite 200
Bloomington, IN 47403
www.authorhouse.com
Phone: 1-800-839-8640

First published by AuthorHouse 2/19/2009

ISBN: 978-1-4389-4686-3 (sc)
ISBN: 978-1-4389-4685-6 (hc)

Printed in the United States of America
Bloomington, Indiana

This book is printed on acid-free paper.

CONTENTS

Acknowledgements   vii

Chapter 1:   I Can't Believe I Got This Great Job   1

Chapter 2:   You Don't Have to Be Big to Be Tough   5

Chapter 3:   Don't Forget the Guy Next Door   11

Chapter 4:   Don't Be Presumptuous   17

Chapter 5:   Who the Hell Ordered This?   23

Chapter 6:   Give It a Chance   33

Chapter 7:   This Dog Won't Hunt   37

Chapter 8:   Make a Great Big Pile   41

Chapter 9:   George's Chapter   45

Chapter 10: Allow the Customer to Assume Ownership   51

Chapter 11: Could I Write This Up?   57

Chapter 12: The Cheapest Man   63

Chapter 13: Kicking Butt and Taking Names   69

Chapter 14: Make It Happen   75

Chapter 15: Don't Point   81

Chapter 16: Dumb Questions   85

Chapter 17: They've All Got a Story to Tell   91

Chapter 18: Showtime   97

Chapter 19: Don't Be Afraid of Circles   105

Chapter 20: Rules   113

ACKNOWLEDGEMENTS

I indeed want to dedicate this sales and marketing book to my wife, Jill, who has tolerated my late, long hours and forgiven me for most of my mistakes.

She supported my efforts and was such a dynamic force in raising our two great kids, Chip and Montica and she celebrated with me in my accomplishments. I thank Chip & Montica for all too often sharing me with the rest of the world.

I also must thank God for giving me the drive, creativity, and energy to conduct my activities and for watching over me every day and providing safety over those millions of miles.

I must also acknowledge my many great customers and thank them for their business, as well as all my co-workers who gave me a hand through all these great years. I must also say thanks to all the Sales Reps., Suppliers, and Manufacturers who supported my efforts and ideas.

I CAN'T BELIEVE I GOT THIS GREAT JOB

Okay, you've arrived in the Marketing Department or you've officially been hired as a Salesperson, maybe you've officially started your own business, become a viable part of a family business or joined a regional operation or perhaps a very large corporation.

It doesn't really matter; you are there, so make the most of the opportunity.

Long ago and far away there was a time when one took a position and stayed the course until retirement. This is when they gave out gold watches and had big retirement parties. The honoree was toasted for being the true and faithful servant and recognized for their accomplishments.

As time passed, owners, managers, and Board of Directors separated themselves from those below, and the sense of belonging faded away. Out of this grew distrust, a sense of not being "in the loop," and along came "I'll hang around for a while and see what happens" or the old "till I find something better".

This is the big reason why businesses fail and why good businesses don't become (or remain) great businesses, but more importantly it's why individuals don't achieve greatness in Sales and Marketing.

The thing is ... Be Committed. Be committed to yourself and your employer. If it's your own business you'd dang well better be committed.

If you take a job or start a project, be the best that you can be. If you find down the road that this place or position isn't for you, you will still have more trophies in your trophy case if you go all out while you are in the position.

Companies come and companies go, but it's you who put that great product on the market in '98, it's you who introduced the great ad campaign in '02, or it will be your company that discovers the better way of doing something in 2014.

It is you and always will be you, so take this job and love it. Be committed, because at the end of the day it's you who must be satisfied.

The customer you create today will still be your customer in another sales life if you move on to something else. Who knows—if you give your position your best, the boss, the manager, the owner, all may change, and you may end up staying the course and moving up. It will be you achieving the greatness, and when you drive up the driveway at the end of the day you'll know you are the king.

If you find your situation unbearable, then be looking to move on, but don't find yourself having constant pity parties. Do your best while you're there, and leave with your dignity, and don't leave without having somewhere to go.

Notice that I haven't yet mentioned money or tangible rewards. These will come as they come, it's your mind and heart that have to be in order.

Once I tackled a position of Sales Manager to help a guy rebuild a family-owned business that had fallen into great disarray. We set out to make money the first year, and we did make a nice profit. It was done the old-fashioned way: good service, fair prices, and creating new and rebuilding good customer relations.

The second year we succeeded in getting all the old customers back plus a bunch of new customers. We offered some "cutting-edge" services and new marketing concepts, and by the end of the second year we had made more profit and had conquered the world.

Funny thing is, I had not received what I had been promised, and I saw that the light at the end of the tunnel had been turned off. By not receiving my just and promised reward I knew it was time to move on, knowing that I had done a great job.

Three years later, another wholesale distributor, one that had previously been a minor competitor, came to me needing the same type of rebuilding. I embarked on a journey, again in charge of sales, and again we arose from the ashes and achieved greatness. A lot of this success was owed to the customers I had developed with the first business.

So believe in yourself, be true to yourself, and value your job. If and when the day comes that you must move on, then you have your name and accomplishments to take with you.

CHAPTER 2:

YOU DON'T HAVE TO BE
BIG TO BE TOUGH

Further along in the book you'll meet a guy named Tom who sells good used vehicles, and his long suit is Jeeps. He's a long way from being big, but through his method of product display he projects the image of being big.

There's a hardware store in central Kentucky located along a busy highway in a town of approximately 3,000 people that does a fantastic business in Radio Flyer wagons. This is the wagon you had as a kid, as did your kid, and your grandkid has or will have very soon. This is an established wagon in the marketplace and comes in countless sizes. The retailer I speak of has been around for years and sells these wagons year-round. They have a very visible Radio Flyer display in the front of the store. Folks stop by in the summer and pick up a wagon for someone's Christmas present.

This retailer isn't a supercenter, just a very good hardware store that is a supercenter for Radio Flyers. They have just taken a good thing and exploited it. Come to think of it, if one goes inside the store you'll find that they have every possible part for a chainsaw. If you want to can some vegetables or fruit, they exploit this situation

5

by having all the jars, lids, and pieces for canning. Try to find these at the big store down the road.

Wait ... did I just use the word ..."Exploit"? It's not an ugly word, nor is it an antiquated word or action. You just exploit your strength(s). TV stations do it all the time. They possess an individual who is dang good at telling the news, weather, or sports, and they promote sometimes their entire station around this person, because folks know, like, and respect this individual. The station may not be number one, but they have this Bob or Sally, so they promote to the highest level and maintain a good following.

Occasionally if this lady is drop-dead gorgeous or if this guy is quite handsome, the station goes with a "pretty" promotion, because they know that a large group of their viewers are doing just that, viewing, as in staring at the person and not even hearing what said he or she is saying. I recently was watching a network newscast featuring a quite attractive anchorwoman. Twice she switched to two female "on the scene" reporters. Each of them was more attractive than the anchorwoman. I thought I was watching an episode of The Bachelor. They had my attention, and I don't remember what they were talking about.

Radio stations discovered the concept of exploiting a good thing years ago. They knew (and still do) that if so-and-so is on the air life is good in the community, even if their station is not the overall best.

There's been a lot of rhetoric over the past few years of how a superstore put the little guy out of business. Only time will prove whether a store was pushed out of business or just packed their bags and headed south when the superstore came to town. Many stores have been quite successful existing right in the shadows of the superstore. These stores just evaluated their positions, went with their strengths, and even became more successful. Everyone can find a niche.

Right in the middle of all the Big Boys selling appliances in Louisville, you'll discover a group of local appliance dealers whom were around before the Big Boys . These dealerships still kick butt and take names. Seems as though these businesses discovered that you can maintain and build business if you assist the customer with his or her needs.

Notice the war in the grocery business. These big boys have knocked and banged so much that they've had to cut cost by eliminating their meat cutters and selling shipped-in, pre-packaged meat. Wonder if this is where the guy with the meat store cutting meat the way you want it really kicks his business into a higher gear.

With all the giant grocery stores, each with a large produce area, do you wonder why there is an increasing number of local produce stands?

I know a very good Ben Franklin store that over the past fifteen years has drifted more into selling craft supplies. This business is anything but a price-cutting store and yet will sell more craft supplies before noon than the big boys will sell in a day or two.

If we are selling to accounts whom are attempting to exploit their strengths, it's up to us the Salespeople to assist these stores in recognizing their strengths.

I can take you to three rural businesses in Kentucky and southern Indiana that have become dramatically strong in selling metal siding and roofing. I'm not talking about the shiny stuff Uncle Bill had on his cattle barn when you were a kid. I'm talking about the state-of-the-art metal available in almost any color you desire, the modern stuff you see on schools, churches, businesses, and yes, even homes. These businesses recognized an opportunity, and none of the three are operating out of a super structure. Heck, they are so good I'm not sure they even advertise.

Let's flip it around and talk about the wholesale business. If you are a smaller wholesaler, how do you compete with the larger competitor? How about being intelligent, trustworthy, and able to deliver in a timely manner at a fair price? It also doesn't hurt that your salespeople drop by a little more often than the larger competitors do, and when they do stop, they have a real purpose. Maybe your people make more in-person visits while the larger guy has salespeople doing more phoning, faxing, and e-mailing. It will be a long time before personal sales calls go out of style.

If the small guy wants to be involved and be more visible, he or she can be active in trade associations or even sit side by side with the big guy on the association's board of directors and on committees. There's room for both.

I don't mean to imply that the Big Guy is bad; I'm just saying that a little guy can survive if he or she finds the niche.

This chapter is timely because more Home Based businesses are popping up all the time. All sorts of small businesses are also starting up. This is partly because the big guys don't pay real well, and employees are starting up smaller businesses and home-based businesses in order to support their families. Also, the big guys, in their haste to get bigger, are leaving many opportunities behind, and some observant individuals are finding these opportunities.

CHAPTER 3:
DON'T FORGET THE GUY NEXT DOOR

My first job after college was that of a retail store manager in western Kentucky. On occasion I purchased some product from a distributor in southern Indiana. This distributor had created a customer base in several states and had delivery trucks running for miles in all directions. I later found out that this distributor never called on a very good dealer in Kentucky and just across the river to any great extent.

The lesson here is to draw a "holy circle" around your base of operation including some logical measure of distance. This holy circle is a most logical factor. You then concentrate on the business in your own backyard. The economics are that you don't travel as far, and if you treat the customers properly they will even develop a desire to come to you and pick up product from time to time, further eliminating your delivery expense and speeding up your service. These customers inside the holy circle develop this habit because You are their supplier.

Once you have positioned yourself locally you can add another circle and begin an expansion program. All you are doing is growing your business on solid footing. Don't expand the initial holy circle; keep it sacred, and don't lose your perspective of the business from this group of customers, it can be sizeable. As you develop new real estate coverage and service areas, the expansion process will help to develop solid business and keep the competition at a distance. This program is much preferred to a helter-skelter attempt to grow.

I know a great grocery store manager who doesn't have the lowest prices, but he is obsessed with supporting the nearby schools, cheerleaders, dance teams, athletic teams, and groups serving kids, especially kids in need. His store does great business, and many of his customers shop with him because as the manager he takes pride in serving his local community. One just doesn't mind paying a little more from time to time when part of the money is going back into the community.

Another example is a local guy with an ice cream business who sponsors countless Little League teams in every sport. He totally covers the board right in his community. There's always a crowd at his business all year round made up of folks of all ages. Wonder why?

Once, while working with a major mass merchandiser, I was offered the opportunity to become Department Manager for a new department for Large Appliances. This was a totally new concept for this business, and we were the only such outlet for this mass merchandiser for many miles. But we were not without competition because that number exceeded sixty competitors in the immediate forty miles.

The system was set up not without problems, but it worked rather well as a whole, and I had two fantastic guys assisting me. During the first year we sold appliances into eleven different states, as deep as 200 miles into Kentucky, Indiana, and Ohio and even twenty-six miles away in our own county. But 18 percent of our sales came from our own zip code area and another 39 percent from the six next closest zip codes, meaning that 57 percent of our business came from our holy circle. To back up to a previous point relating to our holy circle, we offered a very good home delivery service, but 34 percent of our business was "cash and carry."

When establishing your "holy circle" of operation, it should be done in a logical "route" fashion. You can send out salespeople and mailers, and once you're acquainted with the prospects you can sell a lot over the phone. But a good driver and a good truck can only cover so many miles in a day. So, daily routes should to be set up to maximize efforts and profits.

Sometimes growth needs come along, as a good salesperson will find a pocket of business in a new geographic area where he or she can satisfy many needs. This area may be outside your established operational areas. If so, go get the business. Set up an expected delivery or service schedule and ensure that the salesperson continues to service these accounts and seek more customers in the new frontier. Satisfied customers talk to other possible customers, especially within a given industry, which benefits the suppliers and the salesperson.

I know a wholesale distributor who, once upon a time, had a good following nearly 200 miles away in North Carolina, Virginia, and Tennessee. This pocket of business had eroded down to nothing.

So the decision was made to send a salesman over to that area to see what was going on. The salesman came back in a few days with a whole pile of orders, and the phone rang for a week with comments like "I heard you folks had a salesman over this way, and we would like to purchase also. When's the truck coming?" This venture developed into a semi truck load a week, a two-day trip. Logical new business had been developed.

Now the tricky part comes into play. For economical and growth reasons you decide you want to set up an "outpost" or an area warehouse in order to more easily service an area away from your normal shipping point. This is not a virgin trail through the wilderness. It is a well-traveled road, and there are bodies, overturned wagons, and scenes of mass destruction everywhere. I always heard that the road to Hell was lined with good intentions, and this could be the same road.

We're talking about Economics of Scale, personnel, physical equipment, and commitment. If any part fails the operation is just another cross on the side of the road.

On the other hand, find the key location to best service the area logically and economically. Be careful not to just rent or lease a building from your old buddy or just because the price is right. This could put you fifty miles, 300 miles or whatever off of the logical course. Get a great phone person (forget the modern-day "listen to the message and punch the option because we don't really care about you") and a quality bookkeeper; make sure the salesperson(s) is trained and committed; keep the rent low; do the right thing for best shipping; get great drivers; keep the inventory very practical;

and don't be afraid to shuffle inventory from one warehouse to another and work the area hard.

If you do this well, then you have a new bunch of guys next door, and a new holy circle is developed.

Do this the right way, and I promise you that a competitor will try it, and they will fail because they will leave out one or more of the basic ingredients just because they want to short-cut or out-guess the process.

If you think that my thinking is much too archaic because we are in the electronic future, well, the deal's the same; if one is to venture into other countries, Mars, or even Pluto, the only major difference is the fuel bill.

So, sell to the guy next door, create a Holy Circle, and don't be afraid to add an extra circle, and follow the business and make a profit.

CHAPTER 4:

DON'T BE PRESUMPTUOUS

I always remember the story (and from all indications, a true story) I heard several years ago concerning a dealership in a Tennessee city that sold semi trucks, a "new" and "very prominent" brand. A gentleman drove onto the lot one day in a less than beautiful pickup, and when he stepped out of the truck it could be seen that he wore bib overalls and an old hat. As he approached the showroom the old professional salespeople vanished into the woodwork, leaving a young salesman with the honors.

The young salesman gave the gentleman the full three-dollar tour of the new semi tractors then treated the gentleman as if he were someone important. The man purchased two new tractors, paying cash out of a wad of money tucked away in those overalls. Turns out he ran a successful logging company and hadn't bothered to tidy up before he came to town. Just wonder how the expert, experienced salespeople felt about that deal.

While I was a sales rep with a large international chemical company I had the extra duty of training new sales reps for a week. Once I had to give a young rep a less than desirable evaluation because she said repeatedly that she could never suggest to a customer to purchase a new product for every acre he or she operated. When a quality company spends millions over a twelve-to-fifteen-year period in research proving to the EPA, land grant universities, and everyone else that the product works, that it is safe for humans, animals, and the environment, and it will actually save the producer money, you don't just say "Mr. or Mrs. Customer, would you like to try a jug or two?" I call hers a case of Reverse Presumptions.

When I was blending four part-time ventures I encountered a couple of energetic, hard hard-working brothers from northern Ohio who were marketing Canadian-grown night crawlers. Yes, as in live bait. They were steadfast in their belief that their night crawlers, packed in potting soil in cottage cheese type plastic tubs, could be marketed to convenient stores, displayed and stored in the coolers next to the beer and sodas. Don't presume that won't work, because it did. I sold a bunch of night crawlers to convenience stores in the city, suburbs, and rural areas.

Don't presume that you can't do such a job, because you can. It's a great second or third job for night or early morning. You just don't want a Jeep-load of those guys left when the sun comes out in the summertime. Many people go fishing early in the morning or in the evening, so you just set up some stores, do a "milk run" type of delivery, and just keep looking for new customers.

My greatest "kill the presumption" incident relating to the night crawler business came one day when I was looking for a new customer. I stopped at a convenience market on a very busy highway on the west side of Louisville. I grabbed a container of night crawlers and went inside. I had to wait my turn, because a nicely dressed young lady was making a sales presentation to the owner, her daughter and the lady who managed the market . The products she was presenting were neat displays of bows, necklaces, and similar items that girls and ladies might wish to purchase.

These three ladies flatly turned the young lady down, and as she packed up her materials and left the store, I thought, "If three ladies turn down a young lady who is selling items for girls and ladies, wonder what's going to happen when I put these worms on the counter?" So it was my turn, and I placed my container of night crawlers on the counter and made a minute-and-a-half presentation, and the ladies had three questions. How many can you leave today? How much do we make? And how often will you come around? They became very good customers, and I found them through Sales and Marketing processes known as PROSPECTING & COLD CALLING.

As far as owners and management of companies and businesses are concerned , I am absolutely amazed by the common presumption that if a salesperson is fifty-five years old, or so old that rigor mortis has most likely set in. They feel that the thing to do is to dispose of such people and hire a new person. The reality is that the company or business is just attempting to save money and foolish enough to risk their future on such a move.

This is rigor mortis in the minds of the CEOs and owners, and it can and will spread through the entire business. As a matter of fact, over the past fifteen or so years I've been observing this condition, I haven't seen a business that put it to practice have great success. They have all failed, folded, or deteriorated, or will soon and they just don't know it yet. It's not just a "Ken thing"; I know of several qualified salespeople floating around waiting on the opportunity to help make a company great.

Don't be Presumptuous, regardless of your age, in thinking that you know it all. Everyone benefits from a refresher course in Sales and Marketing, and anyone can learn something at any time. It's amazing how much we can learn from our customers and how much we can learn while finding the correct answer to a customer's question.

It's amazing what we can learn from a young, energetic person after we presume that we are older and wiser. When I trained young salespeople for the chemical company I had a sharp-minded trainee with me one week. Late on a Monday afternoon a severe insect plague hit a specific crop over a wide geographic area. This would rapidly cause producers thousands of dollars in losses.

The new rep and I stopped for a coffee while I collected my thoughts as to how to reach all the dealers who had the ability to move product to producers fast, since we happened to have the product to stop the plague. We needed to educate the dealers so they could best reach the vast majority of producers, explain product usage, and relate the message of the product safety and economic importance to the crop involved. Telemarketing was not the answer; it had to be eyeball-to-eyeball information transaction and writing orders on the spot to begin fast product movement.

Pat and I sat at the restaurant table as I mapped out our territory on a napkin and tried to develop a travel pattern to reach the maximum number of dealers in the next four days. I presumed that I had all the answers, but I wasn't having much luck planning the attack. Then Pat spoke up and said that with what he already knew about the product and could read up on that evening, why didn't we divide the territory and reach all the retailers.

Amazingly, we did just that, talking with each other on the phone each evening and relaying the orders to distributors. We helped a bunch of folks solve a problem, and we covered the territory. Lucky I wasn't as presumptuous as to potentially ruin a situation. Guess what—this experience helped Pat develop as a trainee, which is what a training program is all about.

"Presumption" or "presumptuous" … a word or a condition. If you have the word the condition is about to occur. You know you have the condition when a customer turns you down in what seems to be a strange way or for strange reasons. A drop in sales is another indicator. You know the condition is present when things level off for your business or nothing measurable is occurring in your career.

Presumption … let's analyze this "killer" disease of Sales and Marketing people (bear in mind that it can spread to other careers also):

1. How do we recognize it?
2. How do we cope with it?
3. How do we cure it?
4. How many types are there?
5. How do we know when we are cured?
6. Can it reoccur?
7. Why do we refuse to try something new?

How do we recognize it? You find yourself not providing your customers with intelligent answers to their questions. You're not gaining information because you're not asking questions or the proper questions. Maybe you're not listening to your customers' answers. You find everyone else getting all the good customers. You find your career has plateaued. You find yourself becoming a "talking machine."

How do we cope with presumption? First and more importantly, the only answer is that there is no coping. Go straight for the cure, or slide out of sight.

How do we cure presumption? First you recognize and acknowledge the situation and begin correcting one bad habit at a time. The cure comes when our minds open to capturing new ideas again and rekindling the lust and desire to try anything. Also, we find ourselves allowing the customer to do the talking and spend our time listening to his or her stories and answers. You must begin curing yourself immediately; take the medicine, and do the exercises. You will know you're cured when you begin to think of new ways to solve a problem or present a product or idea. The medicine is Sales and Marketing training, reading, and evaluating yourself after each customer or sales call. You could attend an all-day Sales and Marketing Revival, but the value of that is debatable.

How many types are there? I'm not sure anyone knows how many ways there are to be presumptuous.

Can it reoccur? Yes, at the drop of a hat. All you have to do is close your mind and let the negative events of the day get you down.

If we refuse to try something new, then we can presume that our sales & marketing career is over and that we are headed toward the bottom of the pit because we have disregarded the symptoms, treatments and cures.

Chapter 5:

Who the Hell Ordered This?

I loved this chapter before I even wrote it ....

Anyone involved in Sales and Marketing is speaking an untruth if they say they've never looked out on the receiving dock; stopped dead in their tracks while examining an inventory sheet, or spilled their coffee while scanning a price sheet, because there it is—something that no one claims any knowledge of or being a party to ordering.

But there it is, hopefully not too much of it—no one ordered it, but it must be dealt with immediately.

First thought is: who sells a lot of it? Maybe they need more. Second thought is: who have we not sold anything to lately? Perhaps they are about out. Third thought is: who can sell anything? Here's a new challenge. Fourth thought: cut the price, and get it out of here. And there are other thoughts while a posse is recruited to seek out the party responsible for this blessing.

If the product is pork bellies in a Jewish community, ceramic roosters in a Republican community, or whitewall tires in a Mennonite community, then quick, sign on with the posse, and get a gun and a horse, because the guilty party must be found and made to pay.

I'm sure that down through the ages the guilty party has been found and made to pay for their transgression. But wait, where is the positive side? I think someone wrote a book about making lemonade out of lemons. Well, we're there again …. In my days of selling fine jewelry with one of America's oldest department stores I marveled at the fact that every time a shipment of merchandise came in there was a new group of heart-shaped diamond or diamond accent pendants.

No one up the line ever admitted to ordering the pendants; they just kept showing up. Let's see … how many Valentine's Days are there in a year? How many times a year does a guy need to show his undying love for his lady? And, using the traditional thinking that guys purchase diamond pendants for ladies, how many heart-shaped diamond pendants does one lady need, anyway?

But guess what? Those heart-shaped diamond pendants were reasonably priced, and they were always the great piece to show the guy walking along the display case, hands in his pockets, saying repeatedly "I'm just looking." Truth is, he's waited until the last minute to purchase a gift and doesn't have a clue what to buy. Quick, grab a heart-shaped diamond pendant, and tell him how much every lady would like to have one. Another happy customer, and where's the party who ordered these pendants? I want to thank them for assisting in making another sale.

Then there are the small chest freezers that came in the day before the Easter weekend sidewalk sale when I was managing the large appliance department at the mass merchandiser store. We already had some small chest freezers when this new batch showed up, at a time when most shoppers were thinking about Easter rabbits, new dresses, cooking, and what time Sunrise service was. I ran the department, and I didn't know where these things came from. We stacked these freezers out on the sidewalk so that all the shoppers would pass them. When we prepared to bring everything in on Saturday evening we only had two freezers left. Quick, find out who ordered the freezers, and give him or her some jellybeans.

This mystery product thing is somewhat of a universal problem (or situation). My wife and I were visiting with a bank manager, and I happened to mention that I was writing a book on Sales and Marketing. I mentioned that some of the chapters had interesting titles, like "Who the Hell Ordered This?" The bank manager looked at me for a moment and then began to laugh. She said that she understood, because their branch had ordered a working amount of a specific size of paper, and when the order arrived they realized that there also sat a shipment of some mysterious-size paper that they never used. More importantly, their bank system had no way of taking back such a shipment. Therefore it was time for them to get on the phone with other branches and do some barter and trade for some ballpoint pens or something.

Once in the wholesale distribution business we took on a new line of seed Corn and Soybeans. This very reliable company was going to send us a nice "starter kit" amount of seed to begin this sales venture. I was out visiting customers for three days, and when I returned to the warehouse the place was covered with seed. The total amounted to two semi truck loads. Neither the company rep, his district manager, nor anyone else claimed knowledge of how such an order had made its way through the system.

The seed company agreed to take back any leftover inventory, so we started putting seed in any retail outlet that agreed and gave them 100 percent inventory protection. Of course we all know that a consignment-type program never moves product as effectively as a "paid for" program, because the customer commitment just isn't there, but we sold a little and hauled a bunch back and returned it to the seed company. The situation did plant the idea in folks' minds that we were officially in the seed business.

When I was department manager for paint and hardware with the mass merchandiser it was a new show nearly every week. Just when I had the department looking like I wanted, strange things happened. The department was in accordance with company policy in design and layout, and I took great pains to order exactly what was selling. Then the INEVITABLE WOULD happen. I'd come in early one morning and there they sat ... one or two pallets of something I had no use for whatsoever.

The pallets were marked "Buyer Request" or some other ingenious label, and of course you could never find out who that buyer was. But there's the product .... Naturally this is, in many cases, a generic product packaged differently, maybe not priced much cheaper per unit than the normal generic on the shelf. If it was a name-brand product, the instant thought was that if you had a very adequate supply of Stanley hammers, screwdrivers, wrenches, etcetera on the shelf, why did you need a four-by-four display of them?

The thing to remember is that it's mass merchandising at its best, and nothing goes to the back room. Put the mystery product on an endcap or put the display in the center aisle and it will sell. Just get over the fact that dealing with it messed up your day.

Speaking of mystery products, a very interesting marketing phenomenon occurred with the mass merchandiser. The first of three pallets of generic light bulbs arrived. The most popular light bulb for the American home is the sixty-watt bulb, and that's what these were, packaged in a very sturdy, attractive blue box at twenty bulbs per box. Better still, there were seventy-two boxes on the pallet. No problems—build an endcap, and watch them fly out the door.

The endcap went up, with the overflow going to the riser. A lady purchased two boxes the first hour, and another box or two sold over the next four days. Then the trail ran cold. I moved the endcap to another location, and after a week I moved it to another location. Luckily the boxes were sturdy. Then the inevitable happened. I needed the endcap for something else, so all the bulbs went to the riser.

Luck really happened after this, because two more pallets showed up: one pallet of hundred-watt bulbs packed in sturdy six-packs in green boxes and ten-packs of seventy-five-watt bulbs in sturdy pink boxes. In a moment of crisis, all of these bulbs went up on the riser, and guess how full the risers were looking with over 200 boxes of bulbs up there.

This great opportunity had to be dealt with, so I went to the light bulb aisle, where there were more than enough facings of GE bulbs, and I carved out space on the sixty, seventy-five and hundred watt shelves to put one facing of the generic bulbs in these multi-bulb boxes. I priced the bulbs and filled each facing with six to nine cases depending on size.

Everyday when I came in I immediately checked these generic bulbs in their new location and refilled the empty slots with bulbs from the riser. In less than three weeks this vast selection of generic bulbs, which wouldn't sell on an endcap, were sold out in their new location. I was thinking we could use some more but, of course, it's a one-time deal.

All this shows vividly that if we deal with the mystery product, treat it with respect, and don't price it too low, many times the customer will do the rest and assist us with this unexpected inventory blessing.

These mystery products are a blessing in disguise. They cause us to call on our resourcefulness and creativity and to perform sales and marketing like we've never done or perhaps haven't done in a long time. These opportunities can make a profit, and for one to become desperate in the beginning is wrong and will cause financial loss.

Another way mystery products can help a business is by raising the abilities of the employees and sales and marketing people. Call them together, show them the mystery blessing, tell them you want to make a nice profit and that you want it done in a specific period of time. I suppose if you were desperate you could offer a sales incentive.

During my part-time RV sales days the dealership came across four European-designed travel trailer/pop-up camper type of weird crossbred units. They were strange-looking dudes, and no one claimed responsibility for their being there or wanted anything to do with them.

The sales manager assigned me the job of "dealing" with them as much as time and any willing customer would allow me. He offered an extra seventy-five dollar commission for each unit I might sell. It wasn't the seventy-five-dollar spiff as much as it was the fact that I recognized that the business had space and money tied up in these units, and I was willing to help slay the dragons.

The first thing I did, as time allowed, was to read the instructions and details of the units and translate them into features, benefits and advantages. In a week or so I knew everything about how they worked, and I even passed my knowledge on to the other salespeople. Everyone knew there were four of these units, but I found that there were two of one type and two of another type. This meant that the features and benefits varied and opened up a wider window of sales opportunity. In about a month I had sold two of the units, another salesman sold one, and we, as a group, had robbed enough parts from the fourth one to fix up the other units that the owner of the business sold it to some guy for a show trailer.

There is at least one other slant on this subject. Allow me to use the example of when I started a hydroponics wholesale company with another guy. We had a great growing medium bagged in four-cubic-foot bags. This product had features superior to any other growing medium on the market. It was our first Spring, and we had deposited truckloads and partial truckloads at specific locations. I had one semi truck load positioned at a key location in south central Kentucky. Dealers could go to the site to pick up product, and I rented a truck to make short delivery runs. When you are trying to get a good business and a good product going, you need to work the program hard and with creativity.

One Friday morning I went to the storage site very early and made a couple of deliveries to some willing customers. With much of the day still in front of me, feeling very good about the product and business, I went back to the site and filled the rental truck with 240 bags of the growth medium. My plan was to "store door" the product to other dealers as I traveled up the road.

About five hours later, over a hundred miles of traveling and countless sales calls, finding no new takers, I began to think "Who the hell loaded this truck?" Concern began to overtake me because it was Friday, I needed to get home, and I needed to turn in an empty rental truck so that we didn't have to pay for it over the weekend. I even had other plans for the coming Monday and Tuesday.

Just before 5 PM, I remembered a good retailer in central Kentucky and not too far away who had a safe, rather large dry storage dock. I pulled onto the lot, and since the gentleman wasn't there I ask his wife if I could unload the 240 bags and leave them there for a few days on the dock. I promised to return later the next week and explained why I was in such a desperate position. She agreed, I unloaded the truck, and I took the time to tell her exactly what the product was, what it did, what it cost, what it retailed for, and how much money she and her husband could make if an interested person happened along. You guessed it—in less than a week they had sold all 240 bags and requested another shipment.

The bottom line with mystery products and mystery situations is just deal with them, and try very hard to make a profit. Be resourceful, and sometimes you'll be lucky.

CHAPTER 6:
GIVE IT A CHANCE

How about following the last chapter where we thought that a product had no hope with a chapter of "Oh, come on, give it a chance"?

What we have here is an "every product has a buyer," "every product has a season" or "every product has a time" thought process.

Not everyone with a car purchased a bobbin' head dog; not everyone with a taste for candy likes nuts, and not everyone wanting a car purchased a Geo Metro.

Point is -- THERE IS A TIME AND PLACE FOR A NORMAL SALE AT A REASONABLE PRICE.

The product could be that mystery product that just showed up, which no one admits to ordering; it could be something that was sent to every store in the system; or it could be a product you took a chance on because it looked like a great deal.

Situations like this require new marketing efforts. Build a great display, and make the product look good. Do some research, and find new customers who could use the product. Have the Sales staff dig into the product and find every Feature, Benefit and Advantage, and then perhaps rebuild their sales presentations.

The product could be moved as a RELATIVE SALE …. If your customer will purchase X amount of a traditional product, throw in a couple cases of the "chance" product at a good price.

In the mass merchandiser appliance department I have already spoken of, we mysteriously received two large cases of burst-proof washer hoses. We already had an adequate display of these hoses. This hose sold for nine dollars and ninety-five cents. Each washer, of course, takes two hoses. No problem …. Just sell more washers, right? The only problem is that each new washer comes with two free hoses.

The only thing to do was to promote these extra hoses as offering total security from rupture and ruining a carpet or house. We displayed them so folks knew that value. Perhaps they had experienced such a situation or knew someone who had. We also looked for plumbers and service persons who kept spare parts in their service trucks. And there were always the folks who just moved to town and found that they didn't bring their old hoses with them. After a while these extra hoses went away.

Let's go back to the jewelry department and look at all the Mother and Child diamond accent pendants left over after Mother's Day. These are fine pieces of jewelry, and we must remember that every mother has a birthday. And what about that guy who is at a loss as to what to give his wife for their anniversary? Works great if they have kids.

This book has already mentioned PROPER DISPLAYING about six times in one situation or another. Every product has to be displayed in some fashion; sometimes you'll have to display it in two or three different ways, and it's a pretty sure thing that you'll have to take one out of the box and set it up for folks to see.

You may have to TAKE THE PRODUCT ON THE ROAD to show folks what it is and what it does, sort of like about ten years ago when I was contacted by a seed rep from the southern part of the U.S. He had a real good seed line for livestock forage crops, but his best card was a line of forages for deer and other wildlife. He was making some events, but he wasn't connecting with any potential buyers. He had the product, but he was not connected to the market.

This seemed like a natural situation … great product … half the world was hunting and the other half feeding livestock … what he needed was the market connection.

He contracted me to do the connecting. We traveled Kentucky for seven days. I took him to the RIGHT PLACES and put him in front of the RIGHT PEOPLE. All he had to do was make his presentation. I never was so tired of hearing a presentation in all my life. But he was in front of the players, and he made some sales and created a real awareness for his product.

I'm sure you are familiar with the saying "if it looks like a duck, walks like a duck and quacks like a duck, then it must be a duck." In situations such as this there is a pedigree, proven research, and performance to back up the product. This always helps, whether it is seed, deodorant, SUVs, or whatever.

I always have maintained that the difference between a buyer and a qualified buyer is that the qualified buyer has the money. In my introducing the seed guy to the real businessmen who drove the market, I was also introducing him to the qualified buyers. So we were honestly giving the products a chance.

CHAPTER 7:

THIS DOG WON'T HUNT

Or we could say, don't become emotionally involved with your product.

Now, right off the bat we have started a fight with the folks who say that one must—if not love what he or she is selling—at least have a "sincere interest" in his or her product, idea, system, etcetera.

Let's save the love and affection for the "I Love This Product" chapter in my next book.

Right now we are dealing with something for sale that ...
- Looks like something many consumers would want
- Appears to be something everyone needs
- One would think is the greatest invention or concept to ever come around

Problem is, no one wants it ....

You've done the ads, done the coupons, used all your great sales and displaying skills ... and you still have the product in inventory.

So what do you do? Right, kick it out the door with the first good offer to come along. Be done with it and move on. It looks to be the greatest thing since sliced bread, but the market still wants the bread.

But wait, there's another side to the story ….

When I was Sales Manager for a wholesale distributor I made the mistake of purchasing two pallets of a growth regulator for grass, and we had to dump the product on the broker market. Let's analyze the product:

1. It was produced by a quality company.
2. It was safe to humans, animals, and the environment.
3. If properly sprayed on grass it slowed growth and led to many advantages for the customer.
4. It had application in the landscape, golf course, agricultural, lawn and garden, and maintenance markets.
5. It was fairly priced.
6. It was packaged in a quart container, which made it convenient for any consumer.

There was only one problem: the markets__ rural, urban, and suburban, would not accept the product. No one in a large geographic area wanted the product, so it was a complete failure.

The lesson learned here relates to the lack of market research prior to purchasing. You must establish a perceived need for the product in at least one market.

It would have been great if the manufacturer had not presented such a demand as "You have to buy two pallets in order to be the local distributor for the product." Better still, they could have provided some type of a "kick-off" promotion. Also, there could have been a little demo material for some local performance trials. Come to think of it, I could have requested all of this or declined the product.

Over the years there have been cars, candy bars, beverages, cookware, and all sorts of apparently good products brought to the marketplace and failed. Some of these products just might have made it if a different approach had been taken.

So what does all this have to do with sales and marketing? Well, we just talked about the marketing or the lack thereof.

Some say a good salesperson can sell anything. Sure thing, but we have to define whether the sale was ...

> .... for a nice profit
> .... just above cost
> .... at a loss and may be teamed with a good product in a relative sale
> .... dumped at whatever price

The point in all this is that one must not become emotionally involved with whatever the product or project is to the point of not being able to kill it. Once emotion overrules logic, then it's hard for the salesperson, sales manager, project manager, or whoever to see that there is no longer a reason to put forth an effort, because valuable time will be wasted. What's the old saying? "Fish or cut bait".

While managing the Large Appliance department, one of our first display models was a refrigerator with a bottom freezer with an open-out freezer door …. Great idea and we did everything to sell it. When I left the department over a year later that unit was still in inventory. We even brought in a couple of more expensive models from the same company (and believe me, this was a major brand), and we were using these more expensive units to create the old EITHER / OR sales approach. That's right, the more expensive units sold, and the dog was still there.

In the jewelry department there were these really cool-looking pieces made of Black Hills Gold. No, on second thought, I'd rather forget those pieces, but you get the idea.

Stay with logic, resist the emotion (there's a difference between emotion and enthusiasm), and realize that sometimes that dog just won't hunt.

CHAPTER 8:

MAKE A GREAT BIG PILE

Thus we arrive at a Sales Psychology Graduate Course.

Not too long ago there was an auto repair shop on a four-lane highway a couple of miles from my house. The Gentleman had a very good reputation and also sold late model used cars. He dealt in all models but he had a special attachment to Jeep Grand Cherokees & Laredos.

Regardless of how many used vehicles he had at any given time, he displayed them all very well, but he had a special way of lining up the Jeeps so that whether he had four, seven, or ten, it looked like a near-endless supply. If a person asked someone where to buy a good used Jeep the response would be why not go see Tom, he always has a whole bunch of them.

There is a definite General Public psychology to making the pile big. There is power that comes with the image of having a big pile to the person with that pile. The potential buyer is mesmerized, and the seller has the power.

Let's talk about this power. Once as a wholesale distributor sales manager I had a very good customer in central Tennessee. I was by his place one day, and he was shopping for the best deal on a very popular tobacco growth regulator.

The gentleman was a great shopper, and he was looking for the best deal on a cash purchase basis. I gave him every discount I could, but the price wasn't good enough for him as he sat there with the checkbook open. Then I remembered that I had one more card to play. I told him that if he took a total semi truck load of product I could pass along another five cents per gallon.

He researched his records and found that the most he had ever sold was thirteen pallets of this product. Now he had an opportunity to have the best buy around, but he would have to take the twenty-pallet load. He wrote the check for the semi load after I promised that I would try to help him with a little inventory protection if needed.

Want to guess what happened in less than two weeks? That's right—he called up and said he was sending a check for another twenty-pallet load.

Now how does a half-truckload buyer suddenly become a two-truckload buyer? Here's what happened:

- The simple five cents per gallon better deal gave this gentleman total power over his competition.
- Customers saw a whole truckload of product being unloaded and immediately assumed that this was the place to purchase their growth regulator.

- The lower price gave this gentleman an opportunity to sell to some smaller dealers in the area …. Why shouldn't they buy from Bobby? He had the biggest pile around of the good stuff.
- This gentleman may have assumed a new mental role of being king of the hill because he had the deal.

This dealer also retailed groceries, and this growth regulator experience gave him a chance to witness what an older storekeeper had once told him. This being that if you have ten to fifteen watermelons in front of your store; folks will walk right by them. But if you unload a whole load right in front of the door, and customers almost have to climb over them to get into the store, then you will sell every one of them quickly.

There is a RV dealer in Indiana who uses a TV ad with a panoramic aerial shot of his display lot. This is much more effective than a shot of the front door.

Having a large pile sort of eliminates the hard selling. I know a clothing retailer in Louisville who creates a massive display of ladies' hats in the middle of his store a few weeks before the Kentucky Derby. All the salesclerk has to do is make sure the mirror is clean and not blocked, keep a good supply of hatboxes, and keep the cash register warmed up.

Mass merchandisers do this quite well with seasonal candy, school supplies, Easter bunnies, etcetera, but I also maintain that any retailer of any size can do the same thing by buying at the best possible price and creating an unforgettable display. If the consumer perceives that you are the place to go, then the word will spread quickly through the community.

During a three-year period I had a booth at the North American Livestock Show in Louisville. This is a really big show, and I basically promoted a high quality livestock probiotic. This product could be provided for livestock year round, but it was really good for animals under stress such as show animals.

I had a large pile of cases of five-pound bags, but I also had bolus, soluble powder, and oral paste. I had product for a show crisis and product exhibitors could take home. The word spread through the show that I had what they needed.

As I said before, any business or individual can play the Big Pile Game; just make the best purchase possible, do it with quality product, and have a reasonable sale price that allows you to make a profit. If the retailer is able to do this with a degree of regularity, then he or she becomes the place to buy.

Chapter 9:

George's Chapter

Possibly the best salesman I've ever known is a guy named George Cox. George is notorious all over western Kentucky, southern Illinois, Indiana, Tennessee, and who knows where else. Customers and competition know him and respect him, because he's good, knowledgeable, and easy to like.

George's famous philosophy is ... A PRESENTATION WITHOUT A DEMONSTRATION IS JUST ANOTHER CONVERSATION. When we adopt this line of thinking, be it in Sales or Marketing, we are no longer dealing with "lust," "temptation," coupons, or "let's make a deal." We are now WORKING THE MARKET.

Your new product, which just might be better than an established product, cannot take out the established product easily. The potential buyer who has used the older product for years knows that that product is dependable and worth the money and actually may see this new product as attacking the established product. I have conducted hundreds of demonstration plots and examples to "show and tell."

So, here comes George with his Presentation unloading a whole load of features, benefits and advantages right in the customer's lap, giving the prospect a view of things to come with his product.

But now we have to Demonstrate the product with actual performance. We could be taking impurities out of tap water or cleaning a ring to show its true value, or it could be more elaborate, such as showing how to apply a new type of roofing and observing the performance for a few months.

Better still, get the prospect to purchase enough engine products to use in a vehicle for a year or apply to a new product two-hundred-acre field and grow a crop from start to finish.

If you aren't showing the product then you are just having a Conversation.

If one has lost his or her zeal for Demonstration or perhaps never has had such ability, there are easy ways to perk up or re-perk up this ability. Go to an event such as a State Fair and find the guy or gal with a lavaliere mike showing his or her cookware, a new way to wax a car, or perhaps working with home improvement products. These people do it on the fly from start to finish without commercial breaks.

They aren't too hard to find; they are the people with a large crown standing in total silence and awe. Forget the e-mails, faxes, mailing, coupons or whatever …. These crowds at the fair prove that the potential buyer wants to be entertained and taught and shown the way. It's called Demonstration.

Now let's catch up with George again. I say catch up because he's always a step ahead. I haven't seen him use a lavaliere mike much, but he knows his products, he reads his customers, he listens to his customer (dang, did I say LISTEN to the customer? What a novel idea) and is always prepared to show the customer, not tell the customer, what he or she needs to know. This is good because if the customer is a dealer he or she knows what he or she is getting and can hit the ground running to promote the product. If the buyer is the final customer, then he or she knows what the product does and how to use it.

Once at a regional meeting of the agricultural chemical company sales staff I used to work with our regional manager closed the afternoon session with a fifteen-minute presentation called the Saga of the Empty-Handed Salesperson. He cited himself and a valuable lesson he learned one afternoon as a sales rep.

A good customer of his was located on a major travel route, and he had to pass this customer many times in order to reach many other customers in the area. If time allowed the salesman would stop in just to say "hi," thinking and assuming that he was building extra points in their business relationship.

One afternoon on one of these visits after the initial conversation the customer said, "I see that you stopped by for no apparent reason." Well, the salesman, being entrenched in his relationship-building mentality, was completely taken back by this comment. When the salesman regained his composure he ask the dealer what he was referring to, and the dealer remarked, "When you came in the door you had nothing in your hand."

All the customer was trying to point out was that if the salesman wanted his valuable time he should have a purpose and be ready to "make the pitch," do the "show and tell," or make the moment count.

This example really spoke for itself, and this fifteen-minute story made more of an impact on us than perhaps all the other information we had heard gained the entire day.

I blend this story into George's Chapter because you must gain attention some way before the presentation and demonstration begins. Then make the presentation and the demonstration count.

What's the customer to do if the salesperson gets creative? Jokes and stories of car salesmen experiences abound. What if the salesman walked out on the lot and instead of saying, "I'm Bob, how are you doing?" He had the keys to three of the most popular cars and said, "Hi, I'm Bob. Which one of these cars do you want to take for a drive?"

Or how much salesmanship is left when the candy maker hands you a free sample as soon as you walk up to her work area or into her store? Or when the arts and crafts person invites you to sit down and become the potter at the wheel or allows you to participate in making something?

I told my dealer customers for years that Ciba-Geigy had a great new grass control herbicide coming and that this product would revolutionize the industry and save their customers many dollars. Of course they responded by saying, "Yeah, right," because they had heard other companies make similar comments for years.

When the time came and the product, Dual 8E, was about to be released, I went to Grayson County, Kentucky, and asked a good dealer of mine named Harold to find me a soybean field with the greatest weed pressure, where no herbicide had ever really performed well. Harold thought for about five seconds and then took me to a large field farmed by a gentleman named Bill who had never had satisfactory performance from any grass control product. The gentleman allowed me to use his field as a demonstration plot, Dual 8E performed extremely well, the Demonstration became the Presentation, and Dual 8E was successfully introduced into the marketplace. TV ads are a real asset in product promotion, and well-designed literature pieces are very necessary, but what happened in that twenty-acre Grayson County soybean field put the product on the market for me in Kentucky.

"What does it do?" and "How does it work?" often overshadow "How much does it cost?" I have sold a water purification unit through direct marketing with a quality company for years. You put in a gallon of tap or well water, plug it in, and it perks out the impurities and leaves you with a gallon of pure water. The unit costs $ 425.00 and leaves you with a gallon of pure water costing about fifty-six cents. The water tastes good, and when you show the prospect what was perked out of the water as impurities he or she gets interested pretty fast.

The demonstration also puts into play the old "what you see is what you get" theory.

CHAPTER 10:

ALLOW THE CUSTOMER TO ASSUME OWNERSHIP

The references I made in the previous chapter to a bite of free candy in a candy store, or the potter allowing you to help make the pot or and the car salesman tempting you to drive a car right off the bat are TEMPTATIONS, but they are also part of where this chapter is going.

One morning I stopped in for a short appointment with a Lawn and Garden equipment dealer in south central Kentucky. It must have been the morning for appointments, because another salesman was with the dealer, and another salesman was in front of me. Things had become backed up for some reason.

It wasn't convenient for me to ask the secretary to give me a new appointment so I could move on, so I was just hanging around waiting for my turn. The dealership had a really nice display of high quality riding lawn mowers right in the middle of the room. As I was waiting a gentleman came into the store and casually looked at the mowers.

A young salesman approached the customer, and they proceeded to walk among the mowers. They came across one which evidently

51

was of special interest. The customer stood in front of the unit, and the salesman stood next to it. The salesman showed the customer all the gears and items of interest on the panel, while the customer leaned over the tractor from the front and almost stood on his head to see everything.

You guessed it …. Why not get that customer seated on the seat with his hand on the gearshift, foot on the brake, and eyeball contact with the control panel? Let the customer imagine driving across his own lawn, and ALLOW THE CUSTOMER TO MENTALLY ASSUME OWNERSHIP.

This ASSUMING OWNERSHIP thing was really cruel in the jewelry department. When a lady was looking for a gold necklace it seemed that about 90 percent of the time she was dressed with a neckline that would best show off a nice necklace, as if she came dressed to purchase.

We allowed the lady to try on that herringbone necklace or gold rope assisted them with snapping the clasp together if help was needed, and then we discover why there were so many mirrors in the jewelry department … that's right, so the lady can see how the necklace looks on herself and assume mental ownership of the necklace.

If that's not good enough, let's go over to the diamonds and allow the lady to put that diamond ring on her finger, again showing the side view of the ring on her hand with a mirror so she can see what others would see when she was wearing the ring. Then get out the loupe and let the lady see the inner and total personality of the diamond while it is on her hand. By then she basically owns the ring.

Guys, you aren't immune from the jewelry department lust. Just let me get you narrowed down to two or three watches, and then let's get one of them on that wrist. Yep, you own it.

When I managed the large appliance department an assistant manager of the store came by a few times and looked at a white medium-priced basic refrigerator, expressing that his family needed a new refrigerator. Finally he said that he was sending his wife by and that I should be sure to show her this particular refrigerator.

She came in one morning, and I promptly took her to the refrigerator her husband had picked out. It was not my fault that the large black side-by-side refrigerator down in the corner was speaking to the lady. She was drawn to it, so I pointed out all the features and left her alone to envision the unit in her home. You guessed it ... that's the one they purchased. I'm not sure the guy has ever forgiven me.

Let us reflect for a moment. One of the all-time great sales training course subjects has always been that of HOW TO OVER-COME OBJECTIONS. Not a bad course at all, because many a salesperson or even marketing person has stumbled and even fallen hard at the foot of OBJECTIONS.

The potential buyer usually has objections, and they are ...

REAL:	"I don't get my bonus for two months"
	"I just do not like the color red"

IMAGINARY: "No one in my family has ever owned that brand"

                       "All that caffeine keeps me up at night"

BULL: "We are not really ready to buy today"

                       "We'll have to wait; I'm not sure the cable will reach that far"

PUT OFF: "No thanks I'm just looking"

                       "We'll have to talk it over"

MONEY: "The price is just too high"

                       "I can't afford it"

The list of potential buyer objections goes on and on, and the confrontation is REAL and must be dealt with in a professional manner.

Why do I stick Objections right in the middle of a chapter on assuming ownership? Because the mere and simple act of GETTING THE CUSTOMER TO MENTALLY ASSUME OWMERSHIP will overcome most objections.

My car that I owned and used for company business was advancing in age, as was one of our children, who was advancing toward the age to get a driver's license. I had lusted for a Jeep for years. We had found a dealership that could actually repair and service a vehicle in a responsible manner, not rip us off, and which valued us as a customer. On my visits to this dealership I'd walk around the new Jeeps, kick the tires, get a brochure, open the door and look inside (notice I said "look inside"), and on most visits I'd visit with a specific salesman. But I was always able to walk away, and I'm sure I threw out a pile of buyer objections.

One afternoon I walked into the showroom, and there sat a 1995 white Jeep Grand Cherokee Limited with full-time four-wheel drive. It had been driven by the owner of the dealership for only 5,500 miles. Out of nowhere appeared my salesman friend. He instructed me to jump up in the seat and close the door. He ran around and jumped in the passenger side and began pointing out the advantages, features, and benefits, right down to the leather seats.

As I sat there looking out over the steering wheel the feeling that came over me was unbelievable. I was king of the road. So I opened the door, jumped out, told the salesman that I could never imagine myself owning a white vehicle, and thanked him for showing it to me.

The salesman insisted that I sit down at his desk, and we went over the figures. I saw that I could fit it into my budget. It's 2009, and I still drive the same Jeep with 400,408 miles on it. Its one great vehicle and I knew it was when I got behind the wheel in the showroom and MENTALLY ASSUMED OWNERSHIP.

CHAPTER 11:

COULD I WRITE THIS UP?

The last time I counted there were seventeen known ways to close a sale. That is without conjugating the verbs and not bothering with dangling participles.

Certainly "Could I write this up?" is an approved CLOSE.

What we are doing here is establishing the fact that in Sales and Marketing nothing really happens until someone sells something.

In our sophisticated world of computer cash registers, internet transactions, etcetera, millions of dollars in transactions take place with a guy or a lady standing there waiting to "write it up" once the customer mentally arrives at a commitment point. But there is still an unseen sales agent involved.

Let's talk about impersonal selling. It's done by ...
> ... building a neat, eye-catching display
> ... on the computer it's done through descriptive words and/or photo
> ... in the paper or magazine it's done with the right choice of words

... the inventory must be within the customer's reach and
in adequate supply
... the inventory must be "in season"
... the price must be very visible
... the price must be competitive and tempting

The list could go on, but the prevailing reality is that the buyer perceives a value and blends it with a need, as in "Man, this is a deal; we always use this, and we're almost out at home." The shopper makes the choice, stands in line, makes the purchase, and takes it home ... see you, bye.

To me Internet selling is a throwback to pioneer days. Someone logs on looking for an orange left-handed monkey wrench and finds a guy in Montana who happens to have a slightly used one for sale. Bring in the beads and beaver pelts; the trading has begun.

Another form of sales is the auction. A good auction can be a blast. You can be flat broke and still bid with the best of them if you know when to put your hand down. In all the excitement you can get what you want at a good price or find out later that you kept waving your hand way too long.

What about the open market? In the first few years of our marriage, my wife thought I was awful if I asked someone if he or she would take less for a product. She was firmly convinced that the posted price was the posted price. Then I won a company trip to Acapulco, Mexico, for achieving sales above and beyond my established goals. I took my wife along. I had lived in Mexico on an exchange program in 1966 and was familiar with the market structure, but she didn't have a clue. The entire group of us went to the open market one afternoon, and after about twenty minutes my wife was a "born again" shopper and has been ever since. Don't tell her the big-screen TV can't be purchased for less than a certain price.

Of course there are professionals who achieve a status just because of a degree and specific training and can charge whatever the market will take. We may not like their price, but I can assure you that when I encountered any one of my four kidney stone situations I was in no mood to discuss price with the hospital or my urologist. This also brings up the point that sales and marketing does involve both goods and services.

We've now circled most of the wagons, and it's time to get back to the hard core question, Can I Write It Up?

All the products on the self-serve shelves and pretty end caps got there because someone did some marketing, and someone sold the product to someone else. Many times a retailer has called up his supplier and said, "I'm about out; send me a couple of semi loads." This happens after trust and faith have been established. Trust and faith usually ride in on the shoulders of a good salesperson.

The shortest sales presentation and close I ever heard of was of the salesman who looked in his customer's warehouse, saw that he was nearly out of a product, stuck his head in the showroom door, made eye contact with the store owner, and said "I'm sending you another pallet of 'X' because you're about out." He did, and the dealer sold it. A move such as this happened between two people with a very positive relationship developed over time.

Unfortunately our society is now filled with all sorts of "slime" selling. You see on your phone bill that the phone company has allowed some "no name" company to slide charges onto your account; the credit card company allows a wannabe company to make charges to your account; and there's no telling what happens on the Internet. But the slime will always be with us, and we must keep a constant vigil. Such a company has no quality product and doesn't have the fortitude to look a person in the eye and make a sale.

What about all the folks making the sales presentations, doing the show and tell, building the trust, gaining the buyer's confidence, working the long hours, and prospecting for new business? This salesperson, as many times a day as possible, must, at some point, ask for the order and do it with some type of a proper close. Sometimes it takes more than one close attempt. This all has to be done in the proper manner.

While managing the large appliance center I sold a great refrigerator to a nice young couple. They had been by earlier and I had given them information to take home and study. I allowed them the freedom to shop around and compare, because they truly appeared be in the "not ready to buy" frame of mind. They hadn't even agreed on the color, size, or style.

I have no idea how many appliance businesses they visited, but when they came back they had just been to a home supply/lumber business that also sold appliances, and they weren't happy campers. They had found a refrigerator they liked, and while they talked to each other, their salesman said, "Well, whatever you decide, just let me know," and walked away. Yeah, right—guess who else just walked off and right back to me, the guy with the great delivery and great price who was not afraid to give them latitude.

Some might say that I and the other salesman basically treated the couple the same. The difference is he walked away from them, and I wasn't afraid for them to walk away from me.

If you are going to be a salesperson you have to treat people as humans, develop your skills, be able to provide needed information, look like a respectable part of the human race, and not be afraid of your profession. Have pride in what you are doing, and help the customer make a decision. If the customer has no more questions, then heck, sell it to him or her. Don't waste his or her time. He or she has a house to clean, has to be back to work by 1 PM, has golf to play or kids to have fun with or haul to a game. A customer only has so much time for you to sell what he or she wants to buy anyway, so go ahead, ask for the business and reach for the order pad.

Once as Christmas time was approaching my wife and I decided to purchase a VCR for each of our two children. We took a pen and pad and went forth into the world to seek out these VCRs. After five stores we had all sorts of notes, information, and prices, and nothing related to anything else. We were completely confused. Lucky for us, the guy at the sixth store was all of what I have been talking about above. His price was in our budget, he explained how they worked, and he even told us why he would buy them if he was shopping.

Then he had the audacity to tell us to shop around some more and compare. We pulled out our checkbook and made him go get his order pad, because we had made the decision he had allowed us to make …. So write it up.

CHAPTER 12:

THE CHEAPEST MAN

I consider this one of my basic rules of Sales and Marketing since I've never heard anyone else use the term. The reality is that NO ONE HAS EVER SEEN THE CHEAPEST MAN. I know this must be my own marketing rule, because more than once I tried to be the cheapest man but did not succeed.

The point is that whatever you select, be it ladies' wear, a food product, paper goods, or wiggling pins for wobbling wheels, set your sale price as low as you can go, and then take off another 30 percent. Guess what? Your friend comes by and says, "Cool, I saw them across town for twenty-five cents less."

Sometimes the other guy's price is smoke and mirrors. He quotes a price on a pair, as in a washer and dryer, but he mixes and matches the pair. How about the person who says the unbelievable price is "X," but when folks get there he says he's out right now and doesn't know when he can get more. Of course there's always the "raise the price on the product, then offer a gigantic discount" program. Is cheap really cheap?

Let's say that there's you and eleven other businesses in town who sell the same red widget. You go out and do some comp shopping and find one guy cheaper than you. If the twelve of you each have 8.5 percent of the market, you have to ask how many folks out of a hundred are going to drive around and shop all twelve stores. Chances are it's not a very large percentage.

If your red widget is making you 20 percent gross margin, and that cheapest man is grossing 12 percent, what will you profit by dropping down to meet him? The reality is that if you drop down to meet his price you just lose 8 percent on most of your sales, because your customers are your customers. They rely on you for a smile, or your knowledge, or your location, or your complete inventory, or your store hours, or your eyebrow-raising coffee or something. Chances are you could raise your red widget price 5 percent and not lose anyone.

When it comes to pricing there's also the CARMEL THEORY. I once did business with a businessman named Carmel whose pricing theory evidently was this: if he had 200 units of a product and made two dollars a unit, when the 200 were sold he had $400. He sold several various items, all under the same theory, and when he sold out, if it was still in season he'd buy another batch and go again. If another season was approaching he'd just bring in an in-season item. The program must have worked, because he raised a nice family and had some money, and he evidently didn't go to bed at night worrying about his margin.

Margins are quite interesting. One can have an item costing ten dollars, and if you want to make 20 percent margin you come up with either a twelve dollar price or a twelve dollars and fifty cents price. Just depends on how you punch the calculator, but both are 20 percent margin. In case you don't have a calculator, multiply ten dollars by 1.2 to get twelve dollars or divide ten dollars by .8 to get twelve dollars and fifty cent.

Whether you do it with a calculator or Carmel's way, you'll end up with the gross profit you desire. The secret is having the right product in the right place at the right time. Carmel excelled at this procedure. He was also twenty miles from the nearest competitor, and if you didn't like his price, oh well.

The deal really begins with your buying power and ability. If you can purchase the ten-dollar unit for nine dollars, then you make an extra 8 percent if you sell it for twelve fifty in either case. Do it Carmel's way and make an extra dollar. Saving on operating cost also helps the big picture, as long as you don't cheapen your operation.

When you are into markets such as insurance there isn't the latitude for "cutting deals." Insurance is designed to be a "straight-up" program. The buyer determines the selling price by the options she desires blended with her health status, age, and payment method. In most situations the cheapest guy here is the guy with fewer benefits.

Sometimes money just doesn't add up. I'm reminded of the story of a few years ago in which three guys go to town for an evening of fun and relaxation. They find a motel that has a room for thirty dollars, and they tell the motel owner that they will all stay in the same room. Based on common mathematics their room would cost ten dollars per person.

After they go to their room the motel owner gets to thinking and sees himself as one of those guys just a few years earlier. He calls in his right-hand assistant and says, "I charged those guys too much; take these five one-dollar bills down to them and tell them I gave them a discount." The helper cannot decide how to divide five dollars evenly among three guys, so he just puts two of the dollars in his pocket. When he reaches the room of the guests he hands them the three dollars and the guests are very happy.

So, if the guests get three dollars back, that's about a dollar apiece they were refunded. They paid ten dollars each at check-in, so their individual financial outlay was nine dollars. If we multiply three times nine dollars we get twenty-seven dollars. The helper has two dollars in his pocket, this totals twenty nine dollars, so where is the other dollar?

Does this sound like a bumpkin story? What if the room cost $3,000 and $100 disappeared? Now where's the bumpkin?

I would be remiss if I didn't relate the story of the father and son who had a truck and were purchasing items for fifty dollars each, driving quite a ways off and selling the items for forty-nine dollars each. After three or four loads the father says that he can't see them making much money, and the son agrees, and feels that they need a larger truck. Another bumpkin story …. Could be, but I've seen it happen in real life more than once.

A real tragedy in the whole scope of things is the businessperson who has great skills at purchasing products better than most people, and has the lowest purchase price. But instead of keeping this extra profit margin he or she gives it away, just to be known as the low price guy.

When you put all this together you realize that even though a couple of folks have seen his footprints, no one has seen the Cheapest Man. The answer is to find the right product, choose your course, and try to make some money.

CHAPTER 13:
KICKING BUTT AND TAKING NAMES

I'll warn you going into this chapter that it's not intended to be an autobiography. It's about hitting the dusty trail and looking for business. Some may read this and say that all this is long ago and far away. I beg to disagree. You can sit behind the desk and computer, hide behind the e-mails, phone calls, faxes, and mass mailers, but there will come a time when you'll have to leave the building. You'll have to leave your base of operation and go forth into the world to visit your customers and seek out new customers.

My first job out of college was managing a farm cooperative retail store in western Kentucky. I was fresh out of a seven-month training program and ready to tackle the world. This retail store had been a partnership between two brothers-in-law, and they had fallen apart, and so had the store. The cooperative purchased the store, here I came, and the rebuilding job had begun. I was blessed with great full-time employees and a wealth of part-time help just a phone call away. The equipment and tools were some of the most basic and archaic known to man. The tools and equipment of our competition was light-years ahead of ours.

So it was time to kick butt and take names.

At least a day and a half each week I'd jump in my car, take a different road each time, and stop at every house. If the residents weren't home I'd leave a note. If they were at home we'd have a short visit, and I'd invite them to the store. A day and a half a week my assistant manager would do the same thing on other roads, and after a while we crossed the county line into a neighboring county.

Of course I did all the other things such as coaching Little League basketball, being involved in a civic club, and showing up at everything that was going on in the county and area. After a while the folks we visited began showing up, maybe just to look around at first, but then they began to purchase product. We grew the business large enough in two and a half years for the cooperative to select a site for a new store and make plans for better equipment.

Then I was recruited by the university to become an Extension 4-H agent. The county program hadn't had a 4-H agent in over two years, and there were just over a hundred youth involved. With the help of a progressive adult 4-H Council, a great bunch of parents who would roll up their sleeves and do anything, we involved the community, schools and businesses, over a hundred and fifty adult volunteer leaders, started a Teen Leader program, and grew the number of 4-H members to over 600 in a five-year period. We used every tool available and even invented some of our own.

Recruited again I was, this time by an international agricultural chemical company to continue developing a thirty-county area in and just south, west, and east of Louisville. I was a sales rep working the agricultural, PCO, lawn and garden, industrial, turf, horticultural, and aquatic markets. My job was to call on end users, retailers, and distributors.

The old base of operation was well established, but we went into an era of introducing new products and new methods of handling and selling these products. It was time to hit the road and deliver the new product message. We introduced fifteen new products in just short of nine years. We made enormous forward strides and achieved large sales increases, but we did it with a lot of first-time cold sales calls and a lot of Demonstration and Presentation (see George's Chapter).

Again I was recruited by one of my distributor customers to help rebuild what had been a very good business. We made a lot of phone calls, did some creative marketing, implemented some new and creative ways of handling product, leaned heavily on the old business name and bringing that name back to respectability, and, oh yes, hitting the dusty trail again and visiting customers and potential customers.

Assuming that this job was completed since we had regained the lost business and added new customers, in two years I moved on to become the Executive Secretary of a major trade association that I had been part of for ten years. This was a full-time part-time position, and one would think this was to be a slick and get by easy job. But guess what happened? The industry started going into its first economic destabilizing era such as the non-agricultural business community is experiencing in 2008 and 2009. Major international, national, regional, and even local business began to fail, and the association membership began to dwindle.

When old members go away it's time to hit the road again and go find new members. We also planned new programs, went outside the box and brought in innovative speakers, and initiated new ways of communicating with our membership, and thus the association had a new focus, and the membership grew to a record enrollment.

Since I needed to fill in the full-time part-time association position with other part-time projects, I simultaneously was involved in direct marketing, live bait, equipment leasing, and recreational vehicle sales. Guess what all of this took? You guessed it: hundreds of cold calls and hours of prospecting. Kicking butt and taking names in a big-time fashion.

Then it happened again. I was recruited by a branch of a large national wholesale distribution business to rebuild its Kentucky operation. This business wasn't just in disarray; it was on its way to hell in a hand basket.

The remaining employees were great, and so we established some goals, did what the regional manager wanted, reintroduced the business to our suppliers, and once again it was hit the road and go look for business. This time the business name was tarnished and too rickety to lean on, so I put it on my back and carried it. We improved service and enhanced our inventory, and then we picked up two outstanding salespeople. Then we started doing crazy stuff like having golf outings, trap shoots, bringing on at least one new product line each year, and chasing our competition back across geographic lines. We created market share, took market share, and positioned ourselves as a major force. Yep, we did it by kicking butt and taking names.

I'll list only a couple more examples.

A fine jewelry sale in a department store is an education for someone used to creating his or her own mobility. The most outward mobility can be to tell some folks to come by the jewelry department or send out some upcoming sales mailers. Otherwise you dress pretty, smile, and attempt to attract rather than run off as many of the hundreds of shoppers who come by the jewelry counters each day as you can.

I had to bone up on the products and develop the ability to attract a conversation with a customer just by being outside the counter and cleaning the glass fronts or by looking busy re-arranging a display. I had to become very astute in the ability to greet and begin a conversation with a customer. Nothing really new, just listen, or ask a question and listen to the answer. Basically it was just listen and respond. It must have worked pretty well; I sold over $100,000 in fine jewelry in about a year and a half.

And creating a large appliance department inside a large mass merchandiser with zero advertisement assistance in a twenty-five by thirty-foot room was a pretty neat trick. We learned how to work the crowd that came to the store each day. We used the store PA system as our advertisement tool and sent out a few product sheets to some factories, firehouses, etcetera, in the area—this was our customer contact. We had over forty area competitors, but we had a good product line, and we displayed the units very well. We sold nearly $400,000 in product in thirteen months, so I suppose we kicked some butt.

But what about you? Enough about me.

You must ... be able to recognize a potential customer

       ... be able to do cold calls

       ... be able to do customer prospecting

       ... be able to hang on to an old customer

       ... be able to listen

       ... be very knowledgeable of your product line

       ... be able to use what you have to work with—new tools may be a while coming

       ... be able to make eye contact

       ... be able to talk to anyone—when you start culling customers they start culling you

       ... be able to Kick Butt and Take Names

CHAPTER 14:
MAKE IT HAPPEN

We've all seen the creative drawing of the bird with a frog in its mouth, the frog with a death grip on the bird's neck. My hat is off to the individual who created that drawing. To me it epitomizes taking matters into your own hands, becoming creative, and making something positive happen.

We've all experienced near-success and could almost smell the victory but had to work really hard for the deal. Sometimes the deal was very slow to develop, and we had to use various techniques to reach the final goal. Here I'm also reminded of someone's comment that the word "No" just means that more information is needed. Persistence is also a very necessary tool.

When I was the young manager of the farm cooperative store in western Kentucky, I had the honor of becoming acquainted with a father and son who operated a large farming operation of corn and soybeans and fed many head of swine and cattle. Their needs for chemicals, fertilizer, seed, and many other products exceeded my store's abilities, but there was a large ring worth reaching for, and that was 40 percent soybean meal. This product was used to manufacturer livestock feed on the farm. They purchased this product in hundred-pound bags, and I knew that I had the best system to get the product to them.

Therefore the goal of this transaction was established. Over the next two years I attempted twelve different times to make this sale, and each time there was some type of a "situation" or objection that the potential buyers presented. On the thirteenth try I made the sale. The order was for a fifty-ton railcar of 40 percent soybean meal. Before I left this position I sold them a second fifty-ton carload. I kept working on my approach and finally obtained the order.

While I was with the university 4-H program there were a couple of situations when I had to make something happen. My goal was to make the 4-H youth program available to all kids, and the teachers of a special education school called my hand. These ladies requested a 4-H program in their school, and I thought it was a great request, but my training and the special needs of these kids exceeded my abilities.

Then the light bulb came on. I was a strong promoter of involving teenagers in the program to assist other kids. I knew of three young ladies, high school seniors, who weren't veterans of 4-H but were very mature and were interested in working as teen leaders in some way. I introduced these youth to the teachers, kids, and the opportunity. They had the knowledge, compassion, and ability to make this project work for this group of kids. They and the teachers planned the program and carried it out, and I stood back out of the way.

Another 4-H program experience involved an exchange program. In the north end of the county there was a rather tight-knit community full of high-achieving 4-H kids. The older high school youth knew that I had once represented Kentucky and the United States to Mexico on an exchange program. These youth came up with the idea that they would like to do an exchange trip with another state.

I mailed out some feelers to various states and almost instantaneously received a strong and positive response from a county in Wisconsin. I took the proposal to the county 4-H Council, which could not see how such a program could help the county. The parents on the council from the north end of the county raised issue with the larger council, so the council basically said we could do it but they would not endorse it. The parents and kids got busy and planned the entire exchange with me playing minor roles. Twelve kids from each state participated, with our kids and adult leaders driving up there first. Then they came to our county two weeks later.

You've already figured it out, haven't you? The next year when a county in Oklahoma displayed interest the Council and kids from all over the county became interested, and about twenty kids participated.

While with the chemical company I devoted an extensive amount of time to our lawn and garden product line, which was very complete but much smaller than competitive lines. One Fall the company developed an advertising program and announced that they would give the dealer a few cents per case for all Early Order purchases to use for advertising. We had a nice Fall booking, but no single dealer had a massive amount of purchases, so the advertising thing was about to go unnoticed. What can you do significantly with seven dollars and fifty cents if you are a dealer looking to promote a product?

Then as if on cue, a saleslady for the leading TV station in Louisville called me up and wanted to meet for lunch. She told me of a problem or challenge with which she was confronted. Her station had a radio lawn and garden guy whom they wanted to build a call-in TV program around. They had given her the account and program to sell and create. Funny thing was, she couldn't find any sponsors.

I ask her how much a quarter of the sponsorship was and went home to do some thinking. I got out the calculator and added up all these small amounts of advertising money that were about to go to waste. I discovered that I had enough money in the collective pile to buy a quarter sponsorship. I then contacted several dealers and obtained their permission to spend the money and I called the saleslady and told her of my discovery. She then went back to some other potential sponsors, and when she told them that my company and product line was in for a quarter sponsorship, the first three contacts she made jumped in also. Thus a long-running lawn and garden TV show was born in Louisville. We made it happen.

Here we need to revisit an example mentioned in the "Kick Butt" chapter. During the mid 1980s, while I was full-time part-time executive secretary of the trade association, the vast economic destabilization period hit our industry. After over thirty years of upward spiraling economic growth the wheels began to come off. Dealers, distributors, and manufacturers, local, regional, national, or international were all affected.

There was a rash of closures, mergers, and sellouts. The association membership was in vast disarray and declining significantly. However, the need for our association was very significant to the industry of

Kentucky so we had to redefine what we were all about so that we could unify our members for whatever the need.

It was actually quite easy. We needed to have periodic meetings, but our programs had to be much more meaningful. We brought in business owners from other states similar to our membership who had already changed their business structures in order to survive. We brought in other businesspersons who had nothing in common with our members, but who had successfully restructured their businesses to meet new challenges. We went "outside the box" to gain needed information.

We revisited our state and brought in many new members who had not chosen to be part of a state association previously. We revisited our needs and found ways to meet upcoming industry regulations and laws. We went forward to find ourselves.

As a result of all this our association looked a little different, our programs certainly weren't as "cut and dried" as before, and we involved new people and more members. We made it happen.

As for sales and marketing, once the national president of the agricultural chemical company I was working with decided to create a President's Club. Each salesperson was given goals at the beginning of the sales year for five products as well as an overall dollar goal. If we reached all six of these goals we, along with our spouses, would go to this far and distant resort and be part of the President's Club.

The trick was to not forget all the other products in our product line and at the same time attempt to gain sales of these five products and the overall sales goal. Plans had to be made; sales meetings and promo money had to be spent more wisely with the dealers and distributors most vital to these sales. These dealers and distributors had to be taught to think like me. It wasn't all self-serving, however; these dealers and distributors set up goals with us and received awards also.

I have spoken of products, programs, ideas, and projects in this chapter, and there are no real secrets. It's just having the will and drive to enhance your knowledge and allow yourself to make it happen.

CHAPTER 15:

DON'T POINT

I have a theory that the larger the store, the greater the tendency is for the salespeople to point.

The customer asks the salesperson if the store sells little green whatever's and where they are located, and the salesperson lifts his or her arm, extends the trusty finger and says, "over there." So all the customer has to do is follow the bright beam of light that flows from the salesperson's finger, and bingo, the customer finds the little green whatever's.

When we deal with mass merchandisers we have to be aware that quite possibly the salesperson has already walked ten to fifteen miles that day and will be lucky to survive until the end of the shift, so he or she just points. Large grocery stores also have this problem. I say "problem" because they, in the end, will survive from what the customer takes or doesn't take through the checkout lane.

Smaller stores have the problem also. It could even be a mom-and-pop business, and mom or pop is really busy doing three things at once, so he or she just points. Again, just follow the beam flowing from the finger.

The opposite of this is that time recently when you asked a salesperson where the little green whatever's were, and he or she dropped what he or she was doing, perhaps even grabbed you by the upper arm, led you to your goal, and perhaps even placed one in your hand and instructed you how it worked. You will have to agree with me that this is a very exciting experience. You felt warm inside, and possibly your eyes even watered. You got so excited that you thought of something else he or she could guide you to, and had you not snapped to your senses you would have maxed out your credit card. If you did encounter this experience you most likely told folks about it for days.

If you are the salesperson and lead the customer to a product it is almost a guaranteed sale. Unfortunately for the caring salesperson in all too many cases, the business does not reward for sales increases and happy customers. But you, the caring salesperson, can make folks happy and develop habits to take with you to another job or career. Remember Chapter One.

Once I was shopping for Christmas gifts for my wife. She had expressed real need and desire for a bathrobe-type garment. I sort of placed a high priority on this item, and as I unsuccessfully went from one store to the next it became a quest. As I walked through the mall I came upon a rather large Victoria's Secret store and I entered. I'm not a very bashful person, but by the time I made it past the first half dozen bra and panty displays I realized that I was a stranger in a far and distant land.

Then it happened: a very nice and professionally dressed young lady appeared out of nowhere and asked how she could assist me. I told her of my quest, and she led me deep into the interior of the store and turned me over to a second young lady, explaining to her what I needed. Within moments I was shown several choices and I made a selection. Heck, the saleslady even walked me back to the checkout counter and wished me a happy day. Funny, she did that— I'd already been happy for fifteen minutes.

If you are a store owner or manager, imagine a lady coming in and asking if you have any green annual flowers with large white blooms. A clerk or salesperson escorts the lady to the proper area, shows two or three choices, and even places a healthy plant in the lady's hand. Wow, all sorts of things take place. The lady feels wanted and appreciated, she is given the opportunity to assume ownership, all she has to do is make an "either / or" decision and be led to the checkout counter after deciding whether she wants two flowers or three. On the way the salesperson also presents the lady opportunities to purchase potting soil, a garden hose, etcetera. Send a message to the checkout counter: "Don't blow it; here comes a satisfied customer."

What if the lady went to the grocery and was in the produce area shopping for a head of cabbage, and the produce manager or even a worker came along and showed her where the fresh items were and maybe even assisted her in selecting just the right one? Or perhaps she went to the store's deli, and the clerk offered a nibble of a new brand of meat to sample. Just a couple of employee actions such as these could seal this customer's business for a considerable period of time. Do this enough, and the news spreads rapidly.

I must offer up a thought relating to the "lone wolves" of our society. They aren't impressed by a clerk pointing, but they also want no interference as they do their shopping. This person's mode can be read really fast by a store employee. Sooner or later these individuals will need assistance, so just usher him or her to the spot and ask if there is any additional assistance he or she needs.

There was a hardware store in my town that had basically anything a person needed. Going there on Saturday morning was somewhat of a social event. No one in that store ever pointed. They closed up when a larger store moved in down the road—or maybe they just wanted to retire. They had a warm and welcome atmosphere. The larger store was very cold and full of just employees.

A lot of businesses go out of business when the larger store moves into town. This, in many situations, happens because they didn't embrace their customers in the mental sense. Some folks find it hard to believe that showing the customer that you care is a form of selling.

CHAPTER 16:

DUMB QUESTIONS

I begin this chapter with the opposite side of the subject, which is "LISTEN, REACT, LEAD & SHOW. Bear with me as I relate this true story.

It's Saturday afternoon, and I'm hanging out under the salesman's tent at the RV dealership. A nice-looking car drives up, and out steps a nice-looking couple and two children. My greeting reached as far as "Hello," and they introduced themselves and told me that they have driven to Louisville from their home in Cincinnati in search of a Coleman pop-up camper. As we were a Coleman dealership and had ten models set up, I led them to the Coleman display area.

I allowed them to look at all the units and spoke only when I saw a need to point out a feature or answer a question. After viewing all the models they chose the second most expensive unit. As I remember it, I said something like, "You've selected a great camper; all you need is an air conditioner." The lady responded by questioning the cost, how it was installed in the roof, its ability to function, etcetera. I answered their questions, and they wanted the air conditioner.

The gentleman then asked, "What does it cost to have one of those little pull-out stoves installed behind that little door in the camper side?" I covered the cost, and he wanted a stove installed.

The lady then asked what the cost was to have one of those cute little spare tires with a cover installed on the back of the camper. They went for the spare tire also.

So the nice family from Cincinnati came looking for a pop-up camper, selected a very nice camper, and with the installed options, went home with a very fancy camper.

Some would call this classic Relative Selling. I would say that I was lucky to meet these folks. Perhaps I was on top of my game that day, but all I did was LEAD, REACT, LISTEN and SHOW.

Needless to say, we are coming in the back door of the original subject of DUMB QUESTIONS.

With my story above I am attempting to say that if one is to be a successful salesperson he or she must …

> … have great product knowledge
> … maintain the appearance of someone the customer would like to talk with
> … be able to LISTEN (I think I've mentioned this before)
> … be able to sell the features, benefits and advantages
> … be able and willing to follow a customer's lead
> … be able to greet a customer properly
> … not ask DUMB QUESTIONS

The DUMB QUESTIONS, I believe, come from a total lack of training by the manager of the employee. When was the last time you heard of an employee taking a sales training course?

In sales and marketing there are some really DUMB QUESTIONS salespeople use even today in our sophisticated society, such as ...

"Can I help you?"
"How are you doing today?"
"What do you need today?"

Perhaps these aren't the dumbest, but let's talk about them. I've heard all three of these greetings all my life and have used them a couple of times myself. Just think: you've encountered this perfect stranger for the first time in the bank, in the farm store, in the department store, at a trade show, or wherever, and it could be the only time you'll ever see them. And the first thing out of your mouth is, "Can I help you?"

I stopped by the bank my wife uses one day to do some banking for her. I hadn't been there in quite a while. As I was waiting in line I heard one bank teller (yes, they are salespeople also) greet each customer with the old "Can I help you?" question. Then it was my turn, and a very nice, well-dressed young lady had just come back from break, walked down to the end window, slid back the little door, looked at me, and said, "I can help you down here."

As I walked toward the window I was so excited and filled with joy that I could not contain myself. Out loud I complimented her on her excellent greeting. It wasn't very hard for everyone in the bank to hear my comment, and as we finished the transaction the manager walked up and thanked me for making the comment so that the other tellers could hear it. This incident happened about four years ago, and I've begun doing some business at that branch also. I look for that young lady every time I go to that bank.

What if your customer is a business owner looking for a great salesperson? Your initial greeting of a dumb early question could cause you to miss a great opportunity, whereas a strong and creative greeting could launch your career. What if you are a business owner and it's a slow day? Your interaction could make or break your store's success that day. Upgrade your creativity and tune up your quiet aggressiveness.

As an example, using "How can I help you?" instead of "Can I help you?" is a change of just one word, "how," from a mundane nothing comment into an expression of genuine interest in assisting the customer in satisfying a need or exploring new horizons.

"How are you doing today?" is just a pure old "good ole boy" greeting, and believe me, the Northern, Western and Northeastern folks are just as good-ole-boyish as the Southern folks with this greeting. If you want to get friendly and cozy with a customer, go to "Thanks for coming in today," followed closely by "I love your shirt" or "I love your purse." Now you are cozy, because your greeting was welcoming and you laid out a sincere complement. So give him or her the tour and show what you have to offer.

"What do you need today?" is an offensive question. If it's a guy he probably won't even respond, except maybe to say that he can find the hammer himself, and back off, because he's not going to steal anything. If the customer is a lady, that greeting will either blow her away or drive her away.

If you feel that your initial greeting should relate to the customer's health and well-being, then just say "hello" or "welcome" and "thanks for coming by today."

It's exciting to see how many ways you are able to use OPENING and CLOSING questions in the initial greeting and even more so as you move through the sales presentation.

Now you've waited long enough: it's time for the DUMBEST QUESTION in a sales presentation. It's as old as the hills and still very much alive today. Here it comes: "How much money do you want to spend?" My mental response is,"None of your business, Mr. or Mrs. Weak Salesperson." In reality, I, the potential customer, will say that I want the best unit at the lowest price.

The burden lies with the salesperson to tap the wealth. Both the salesperson and the customer have the power. The customer has the money, and the salesperson has the product. All the salesperson has to do is get the flow going and listen for the story. The amount of money the buyer has will evolve on its own. (Remember the pop-up camper.)

The customer has zero pressure unless …

> … it's 5:45 and he or she needs something for the party at 6
> … the range died today and she is hosting the Thanksgiving dinner tomorrow

... You're returning from a trip, walking through the airport, and remember that you haven't a gift for your young child

... you can name the rest ....

Oh yes, how can I forget my greatest DUMB QUESTION? I was a junior in high school, and it was time to sell the magazines to raise money for the yearbook. I was looking for the sure sales, so I went into a local hardware store. My greeting was, "Mr. Wright, you wouldn't want to buy any magazine subscriptions, would you?" He looked at me, smiled, and said "no". I was so embarrassed I can't remember if he purchased a subscription or not.

Refine your techniques. I've been rather successful for forty years, and I'm still refining my questions all the time. Ask the right questions at the right time, or keep asking good questions until you hit the right question, when the answer leads to the sale.

CHAPTER 17:

THEY'VE ALL GOT A STORY TO TELL

Remember how I emphasized the word "listen" several times? Well, EVERY CUSTOMER HAS A STORY TO TELL. After properly greeting the customer one may have to ask a couple of open-ended questions, but usually all you really have to do is LISTEN TO THE STORY.

There are a couple of really vital components that are needed here:

- You must surround yourself with quality products and choices.
- You must be knee-deep in product knowledge and/or quickly know where to find a correct answer.

First, let's view the customer coming to you ….

I'm sitting under the salesman's tent at the RV dealership one Saturday morning when I happened to notice a man and woman quietly checking out a new thirty-two-foot Itasca motor home, which was on special. I walked on out to the RV, introduced myself in the proper manner, sat down at the dining table, and readied myself for their story.

They began the story as if on cue. He was a sergeant major in the Army and was two months away from retiring. He had spent twenty years climbing in and out of tanks and was ready to relax and travel. She had been a working mom and had basically been in charge of raising their two sons, who were now out of high school. She too was ready to travel. They said that they wanted to do the main roads and back roads and see our country's beauty.

Logically, it was now time to put him in the driver's seat and let him drive down a four-lane road and then off onto a side road with some gentle curves. We arrived at the parking lot of a beautiful stone church with great landscaping, where we parked and got out to go over the details of the unit in this natural setting.

On this particular Saturday morning the natural environment emphasized the beauty of this motor home, which captivated the sergeant major and his wife. All we had to do was drive back to the dealership and do the paperwork.

The jewelry business also offered up some great stories. There would be the gentleman—actually I can think of three such men— who appeared at the watch counter and said that his watch had gone bad. He had had it since World War II, and it had been given to him as a gift from a special person, be it his parents or a special lady. Each man told the details of how the gift had been given to him and how many batteries he had purchased, repairs made, etcetera. This situation was always addressed by taking him to a name-brand watch, not flashy, but with very basic features. This always accomplished the mission.

About once a quarter a nurse would stop by in sort of a panic because her watch had died, and she badly needed a watch with a second hand and with numbers and hands one could see in the dark. She would always throw out a story or two of how her watch had served its function in aiding a patient. We kept two specific watches so we could offer a choice, and we referred to them as the nurses' watches.

The easy one was the parent or grandparent who would show up with the youth in question about 70 percent of the time and tell the story of how they had purchased Mickey, Minnie, Goofy, Cinderella, Batman, etcetera, but the day had come when the young person wanted a grown-up watch. Girls were no different than boys. Just lead them to the watches, not real expensive, but those with the largest faces, largest numbers, multiple dials, stopwatch features, and on and on. Fancy bands entered the picture, with the girls going for the large leather bands. All this was product knowledge plus show and tell and allowing them to put the watches on their arms.

My next-door neighbor had an ugly old blue Volvo that had about a trillion miles on it. When it died he went down to the Volvo dealer and told them how the car had carried the kids to school, to the doctor, went on vacations, etcetera, through snow, rain, and whatever. Their two kids had grown up in that car. The two kids growing up in the car was what the salesman heard, and he sent the couple home in a new red Volvo convertible.

Many times a lady would come into the appliance center telling us of the sudden death of a washer or dryer. It had been a wonderful machine that had served the family well for years. After two or three repair jobs the end was inevitable. We would listen well, put our hand on her shoulder, show her six models to choose from, and find the quickest delivery date.

Now let's reverse the angle and view the story listening from the opposite angle—that which occurs when you take the show on the road to the customer's environment.

When I was doing leasing with a company that could lease about anything I stopped in on a couple operating a convenience store down on the Kentucky-Tennessee line. After the introduction and a question or two, they began to tell me how long they had been in business, how their business had grown, and the makeup of their clientele. They even told me of how much better they could do if they had fountain drinks, pizza by the slice, and hot dogs. I took some measurements, showed them what these units could make them using their figures, and leased them the equipment.

While I was with the chemical company one of their better salesmen once called me seeking help for one of his accounts. This account was located in west Louisville adjacent to the railroad. The company was in the business of making whiskey barrels. They had a storage lot full of barrel staves and completed barrels located alongside the railroad. The weeds growing on the banks of the railroad and even in this storage lot were somewhat out of control. The real problem began when sparks from the railcars set the weeds on fire. This was not good for a lot full of wooden barrels and staves.

The salesman and the company's manager told me how they had tried all types of liquid soil sterilants and nothing worked. From the information I acquired just by listing to the story, I deducted that the liquid was vaporizing on its way through the many layers of gravel as it tried to reach real soil so it could go to work. I proposed that we use a quality granule soil sterilant in a demonstration environment on the side of the railroad. My theory worked, and the mission was accomplished.

Going into the customer's place of business and fitting into his or her schedule, even with an appointment, blending in with the phone call interruptions, perhaps stopping your conversation while he or she waits on a customer, requires professional sales skills and a large amount of patience.

These skills can come early for the sales and marketing person if he or she involves …

> … Open-ended questions to pull the story fast
> … Using a key literature piece or product sample to stimulate the conversation
> … Using keen observation skills to enhance his or her knowledge of the business

There's a story in what you see, be sure to look around and check out the environment. When you establish the appointment, tell the customer the purpose and give him or her time to develop the story.

It's all right there; just LISTEN TO THE STORY, fill in the blanks, and make the sale or implement the marketing plan. The art of questioning is used to stimulate comments and statements, all part of the story. Listening is where you gain the information.

Always remember to fit what you are selling into the front, middle, or end of the story.

CHAPTER 18:

SHOWTIME

So far in my career I, or I and my co-workers, have had a booth at local home-based business expos, regional Lawn and Garden markets, semi-national Hardware shows, the National Farm Machinery Show, the North American Livestock Expo, the Southern Kentucky Expo, the Greater Louisville Expo, the Kentucky Beef Expo, the Louisville RV show, the Virginia Livestock expo, Kentucky Tobacco, Horticultural, and Fruit and Vegetable expos, and many other events that now I can't even remember. The great thing is that I have a bunch more yet to do.

You have done the same, be it computers, street rods, trucks, cars, food products, clothing, or an endless number of other products. You have possibly also extended from a local event to a national or international stage.

The drill is the same: set up the booth, put out the literature, get out your most appropriate clothing, make up a work schedule, fix up a dish of candy, and get ready to talk to a bunch of people.

But wait—we the booth people have our agenda: tell the world about the virtues of our product(s), line up some new prospects, and make some sales.

What is often forgotten is the crowd, those countless people coming down the endless rows of booths looking for something. That's why they came, to look for something. They want something new to sell, something to solve a problem, maybe this, maybe that, but something. Some come to get the best deals, and they know who usually has them, so they look straight ahead, marching along until they reach their goal, sort of like they have a GPS locked in and the other booths and products don't count.

What if the products your booth offered had that special something? What if the next great thing was introduced to the world at your booth? How do you get the crowd's attention? Booth space and shows cost a lot of money. If you are part of a gigantic company it could be that you don't worry about the cost but act as if it's your company, because if you are focused and sincere you could lock on to a customer who could make your career.

If you are a one-man show you might have all your current expendable cash tied up in that show booth fee, electrical hookup, literature printing, etcetera, and you are also involving your valuable time. What you need now are customers and leads.

Let's set the stage a little more. My wife and I could take a nice trip if I just had a dollar for every "I'll be back" that I have encountered at my booths over the years. They must have gotten lost, locked up, beamed up, or called home on an emergency, because they sincerely said that they would be back. Why didn't they come back? Or better yet, what does "I'll be back" really mean?

- Perhaps something about your booth or your charming personality caused the prospect to stop, but after they stopped they found that they really didn't need any car wax, computer software, carpet cleaner, or investment information. You were nice, however, and they didn't want to hurt your feelings, so they said they would be back.
- Perhaps they didn't have enough money to purchase your bulldozer or finance your franchise, so instead of saying, "I'm broke" they just said, "I'll be back."
- Maybe they only have one or two days to devote to the show and prioritized their time by starting with their primary suppliers, who always have the show deals. After they accomplished this mission perhaps they did actually go back to as many prospects as possible, and they just didn't make it to your booth.
- Could be that you didn't CLOSE or SHOW THEM A REASON TO BUY.

So here we go …. The door is opening, and here they come, potential customers coming down the aisle looking left and then right, sort of grazing like an un-hungry cow. Some will work one side of the aisle and then the other side. Some will even stop if they see something interesting and will ask a question or listen to a speaker.

Point is, YOU'VE PAID YOUR MONEY AND INVESTED YOUR TIME, AND THE CROWD MUST STOP AT YOUR BOOTH.

First you must GET THEIR ATTENTION. I'm thinking that I've about seen it all, from bikini-clad beauties to dancing bears, music and balloons, or register for this freebee or take a free whatever.

Be careful here—some ladies are turned off by the bikini models, and some folks are afraid of bears. The music must appeal to a large cross section of ages and geographic social makeup (sounds like Credence Clearwater Revival or some 60s or 70s music to me). Not everyone wants to register for a free TV; that's more of a state fair thing, Make sure the free stuff counts, and be careful with what you give away. I know a guy who came close to getting kicked out of a show for giving away free salted peanuts in the shell. The event sponsors saw it as a danger and a mess to clean up.

What makes the crowd stop?
- Could be the professional lighting and design of the display
- Could be the way you have your product arranged
- Could be the products you are showing
- Could be that you are a sharply dressed guy or well-dressed lady
- Customers like to touch and feel (not you but the product you promote)
- Could be a well-designed game or participation
- Or it could well be that simple little whatever you are giving away (like the fuzzy little lapel caterpillars the company gave away at the National Farm Machinery Show one year. The ladies dragged their husbands over

a million square feet of display area until they found THAT booth and got a caterpillar).

Once they have stopped YOU ONLY HAVE SECONDS TO MAKE A MOVE.

If you have a game, allow them to participate …..
  If a product caught their eye allow them to touch it ….
    If was because of your greeting then get them to say something ….
      Give them your card, and ask them for theirs (you must get their info)
        Ask them what they like best about your product that caught their eye ….
          Give them a reason to respond ….
            Allow them to not be threatened and invite them to stop back by ….
              GIVE THEM A REASON TO BUY

There's nothing wrong with actually selling your products at your booth. As a matter of fact, having an order pad and pen or a computer screen in the booth makes things look businesslike.

If you are not able to man your booth for a day or two, then turn your booth over to a well-dressed lady. Ladies are eager to talk to businesswomen, and guys will talk to a lady. Just inform her of what you expect and what information you need, and you won't miss a beat.

Follow up on all information you've gained at the show. Do it fast and it can lead to an order; do it slow and you are just a figment of their imagination.

Things not to do at the show ...

1. Don't eat in your booth.
2. If you have coffee, water, or a soft drink keep it hidden.
3. Don't read the paper.
4. Don't always be gone from your booth.
5. Don't constantly be fraternizing with the folks in the next booth.
6. Don't snub the folks in the next booth.
7. Don't have a messy booth.
8. If you are an independent businessperson, don't give away expensive literature that you had to pay for unless the prospect is dead serious.
9. Don't be discouraged by a slow day or a show that appears to be going nowhere; a solid prospect is coming and he or she could be walking up to the booth right now.

Things you should do in your booth ...

1. Be on your feet with a smile on your face and making eye contact.
2. Have a whole bag full of assorted greetings that in some way relate to your product or booth.
3. Have inexpensive yet comprehensive information to hand out.
4. Always have something relating to your business in your hand.
5. If your company has sent expensive literature, give it to any solid prospect.

6. If you have symbolic giveaway items make them readily available to the prospects.

7. If you are tired, don't show it.

8. Serve your customer—if he or she wishes to purchase something, sell it.

9. Make sure you have information to give the "be backs" before they leave your booth.

It's Showtime. It's your show, your money, and your time—make the event work for you.

Chapter 19

Don't Be Afraid of Circles

Don't be afraid of circles; if these circles turn often enough you might make some money.

Straight lines are easy to follow, but they are similar to Fourth of July fireworks: you have to keep loading the cannon to get results. As you have noticed, the fireworks go straight up for a long ways but has to scatter in the proper manner to yield proper results.

I've known a lot of people who, when presented with a circle sales opportunity, would say, "Is this one of those pyramid things?"

Everything is a pyramid: the church structure; government at any level; the military; large, medium, and small corporations and businesses; etcetera. Within these structures no one can do anything significant until it's approved from above, and if someone bypasses the one above, it's suicide to his or her career.

Unfortunately the person who is afraid of pyramids and circles is the person who was dragged to a great "no-name" get-rich-quick marketing opportunity meeting. All you would have to do is draw circles and you would be king of the world. At the end of the meeting they told you the name of the company, and you had already swore twenty times that you would have nothing to do with it. So you left the meeting hostile yet empty and ready to go back and work in the "system." The "empty" part came from the inner self, which knows that you really could use some extra money, and you know that the circles are used by corporations and business every day.

The reality is that some of the best and most quality oriented, some of the most creative, and some of the "value added" products are created and sold by private manufacturing companies. These products sold by individuals are, for the large part, grouped into the NETWORK MARKETING. Network Marketing uses a lot of Circles and it's honest and legal. If one does not know what I mean by Circles, these are circles drawn on a dry erase board to show generations of potential growth if one takes this opportunity and grows the amount of product sold. The more one sells the more one makes. The irony is that I have also seen corporate America use circles.

For those who are afraid of pyramids yet work in them all day, why not look for a company where the sales structure allows anyone to pass anyone at any time? If you are afraid to "recruit" people and afraid to have folks "under" you, then you can at least sell to the end user and make a nice profit. If you are afraid to recruit and afraid to have folks under you, then know that you will never be a department head, supervisor, CEO, or any other position of authority and career advancement.

If you don't want to be involved in anything where the guy above you makes money off the deal, then don't ever go to a store and purchase anything, because that guy or gal and everyone in the pyramid structure above him or her is going to get a cut. What about the company who made the product that the store and the salesperson sold you? Everyone in that pyramid structure, even the truck driver, gets a cut of the profit off your purchase.

CIRCLES ARE REAL. If you draw enough of them, fill in enough names of quality people and geographic locations, and plot a logical course, you will make some honest money. Corporate America does it every day.

Remember the straight line? It can't be straight forever. It has to splatter, take turns, make joints or forks; that's American business. If it stayed straight it would be infinite and go on eternally, and infinity is a long way to go to sell something. I believe it was Yogi Berra who said, "If you come to a fork in the road take it." That's where the real marketing begins. Circles are sort of like wheels, and wheels can take you places.

Enough about corporate pyramids and folks who fear the potential of finding and using a better product. Let's talk about the CIRCLE folks who are making contributions to the American economy.

I have been involved for twenty years with an independent marketing company that came to life in the 1950s with thirty or so products. This was a father-and-sons operation that I believe began in a garage. They made the products and then sold them door-to-door. Can you name any great American corporations that started that way?

Now that you have gone through two pages of paper listing such corporations you can stop for now. The company I speak of made two early decisions: first, to continue creating new quality products, and second, to always sell these products only through individuals. All an individual had to do was agree to purchase the products, pay a small franchise fee, and market them in an honest fashion.

Can you think of any American corporations or companies that used or use franchise fees to expand their marketing outreach? I can think of a guy from Kentucky who made a lot of money with a pretty good fried chicken recipe and helped a lot of other people make some money with franchises. Can you think of others?

The father and sons I spoke of decided that if you were part of their marketing organization, maintained a certain volume of business, and got some other guys and gals involved, they would pay you a commission. The more you sold the greater the commission.

No, wait …. We have two questions to answer:

1. Do you know of one person who owns more than one franchise location? I thought you might. The only difference is that with the company I speak of you don't purchase a new franchise, you just help another person create his or her own circle and begin to make some honest money.

2. Whoever heard of a company paying someone a commission for selling something and expanding growth? Why, that's downright despicable. So I guess that makes insurance and real estate industries and many great American companies and corporations despicable.

Have you noticed a pattern here? Nothing happens until someone sells something, regardless of the item to be sold. Once the sales and marketing process is set into motion multiples are created and the system is born. Someone is in charge, and the delegation and ranking of authority falls into place, be it with straight lines or circles. Thus a pyramid structure comes to life …. It can't be helped. Sorry to the guy or gal who was skeptical of pyramids.

Back to the father and two sons. The products they created were as good as or better than any similar products on the market. Dang, could this mean that if a person purchased one of these products and liked it so well they would want to purchase some more? As in "Hey, Bob, I could use another jug of that stuff if you're ever over this way."

What the heck …. Now we have customer satisfaction and repeat business. Am I speaking of network marketing or a great corporation?

Now if the father and sons help someone else to get set up to sell these products, what happens if someone else #1 gets someone else #2 set up in the business, and in a couple of years someone else #2 is selling more product than someone else#1? It means that someone else #2 is selling more product and making more money.

If you have a chicken franchise and help someone else get a chicken franchise, and in a couple of years that guy is making more money than you, what happens? If you are a distributor of something, say snacks and beverages, and you help someone in another town get set up with the same products, what happens in a couple of years when they are making more money than you?

As an independent insurance agent I get about three mailings or e-mails a week from marketing groups who invite me to join their teams. It's sort of an outreach program, I guess, certainly not illegal or immoral. They just want to make a profit off the business I bring to the insurance companies they are signed up with. I'm a licensed agent with about ten companies, and I could do the same thing, but I'd rather concentrate on helping someone cover a specific need with quality insurance.

We've considered several factors so far and have yet to find grounds of wrongdoing to convict or discipline independent marketing people. They are disgusting, however, aren't they?

1.   They don't have storage buildings ... they use the corners of their garages.
2.   They don't have delivery trucks ... they use the back of their Jeep or custom delivery methods.
3.   They don't advertise .... a lot of marketing is done with word of mouth.
4.   They sometimes get folks together for a sales meeting.
5.   They don't have multiple phone lines and pre-recorded secretary greetings, and they don't have you punching numbers and electing options.
6.   They don't pay taxes .... What a joke. Some of these "circle folks" pay more taxes than some American corporations and companies.
7.   They have a great product and bring it to you. You don't have to park in a ten acre parking lot and walk a tenth to a quarter of a mile to get to the department in the store where there is no one to help you and you don't know what's in the product or where it was made.

We could go on and on with this all day and never really find anything wrong with individually marketed products and folks dealing with circles, so let's give a big cheer to the Conklin, Mary Kay, and other great marketing folks who are contributing to our American society.

Our society has drifted to where both parents have to work to get at least part of what they need and want from life and for their kids. Maybe at least one of them wouldn't have to punch a clock if they were doing some independent marketing. They might just end up with more time for their kids.

Who knows, we might be able to cut into our country's awful divorce rate if some husbands and wives spent time together developing an independent marketing business, having some fun and making some extra money. And each could still have a job.

Another question is… does the lady changing sheets at the local motel have the right to send her kid to the same university as the great American corporate executive does? Yes, she does, and it's totally possible; just find the right products and start using the circles.

The phenomenon is that our American society considers it to be "backward" and "archaic" if we don't…
>   … change the way we teach kids once in a while
>   … change the way we dress periodically
>   … change the music in church once in a while

Yet we conclude in our society that the only way to make a living is to punch a clock as we did a hundred years ago and that we can only make money by working for the man as well as only buying products sold in the store on the side of the road.

The point is, if you want to make some extra money and have some fun doing it, do some research (there are about 2,000 choices), make some choices, check out the dotting of the I's and the crossing of the T's and begin doing something with a few good products.

If you happen to be on the buying end, don't belittle the independent marketing person; they're just trying to hook you up with a product that's most likely better than what you find in the store.

Your view as a buyer or a seller will be from the top, and the view is always better from the top.

It's okay to play golf in your spare time, so it's okay to play with Circles in your spare time.

CHAPTER 20:
RULES

If a Sales person or a Marketing person works for someone else there are always deadlines, quotas, meetings, shows, appointments, and much, much more, all of which crowds our life and blinds us to what's really important.

If one works for themselves everything above pretty much applies here also, except for the self-imposed extra stuff a driven person desires to accomplish.

So, as I said in Chapter One, you have this great position, so do the best job possible.

I feel that there are some basic RULES that we must always be cognizant of and fit into our busy lives.

You are only as good as your last sale or marketing plan. True, my greatest single sale where I brought the check back to the office was $722,000. True, I have helped build and rebuild some great businesses, but the truth is that the world only remembers your last sale, and it must have been rather recent. Otherwise you're just a legend. It's about what you have going right now, and if you don't have a "right now," then go get one. I currently have about twenty "right now's" going on.

It was General Patton who said, "All victory is fleeting."

A. Pray before you go. You've heard of great military leaders who had a prayer before they went into battle, and there are the athletes who offer up a prayer before the game. These two examples are prayers for victory perhaps, but also simply to ask for assistance in safety and having the ability to do their best.

I put a slightly different slant on prayer related to business. There have been times when someone owed me or the company money, or I was going out to investigate a rather strong product complaint; in either case the situation had the potential to be tense. So before embarking on the journey I prayed for level heads and the prevailing air of logic and reason. The prayer was always answered.

It's also legal to pray for your best efforts during the day as long as vanity isn't involved.

B. Don't ever bank on selling to your friends, neighbors or relatives. Sometimes they may work with you, but don't bet the farm on it. If one does want to buy from you, treat him or her as a client—don't turn it down.

I had a friend who purchased a nice piece of jewelry from another salesperson in my department. I had a relative purchase a washer and dryer of another brand in another town when I ran the appliance center. I had a friend purchase long-term care insurance from another agent, and it was the same product I carried with the same company.

You just can't worry about stuff like that. It's much better to do a good job and sell to a perfect stranger. They seem to develop a different kind of a relationship and belief in you. This relationship, in place, they will buy anything you're selling and bring you other customers.

C. PLAN … sort of a self-explanatory word, but it does allude to the future tense.

A great business guru once decreed that we should "plan our work and work our plan." I'm sure you've also heard that we should "get a map and plan your journey so that you may expedite your travel and have a totally successful trip."

Enough about philosophy …. What if the boss tells you that you must sell forty? blue items this month? Develop a plan that can logically get you to the goal, a plan made of all the whos, hows, whens, and where's. What if you only sell thirty three items? Who knows, maybe the boss was thinking that you would only sell thirty.

If your company sets annual goals and quotas, then you have time to really work the market and use all the tools available to reach these goals. Just don't wait until July to begin the effort. I always increase these goals by 25 percent so that I'm always shooting over the top. It is very important to break your markets, territory, and product types down and have goals for each of them relating to the extra 25 percent. Do this for each month as well.

D.   Notice how making PLANS just naturally gravitates to setting GOALS.

Perhaps there are two types of GOALS .... You always hear about those that you are supposed to stick on the bathroom mirror, on the dash of your car, on the refrigerator, or who knows where else. These GOALS are physical or materialistic, and this is you we're talking about. If some type of a tangible carrot dangling in front of you makes you do that, do it. Put these little pieces of paper in your underwear drawer and everywhere else.

The numerical GOALS that I allude to in the PLANS are the bricks with which you construct the year and compare what you need with what you already have.

All GOALS are supposed to be specific, measurable, realistic, and attainable. The two types of GOALS can work together. Review your GOALS all the time. When the time comes to be where you want and need to be, re-evaluate and keep going.

E.   HABITS ... Careful, here's where it gets personal.

I always marvel at the fact that Happy Hour is over before it should even begin, considering that one can work until business closes, and if they are closed here, they could still be open in another time zone. After all the businesses close you drive home, have a meal, spend time with the family, do some chores, etcetera, and then you wonder who went to Happy Hour at 4 PM. Possibly the competitor you just smashed earlier today.

Some folks are condemned for smoking. Could be that the one doing the condemning wears very offensive cologne or perfume. Some folks have a real problem telling the truth, others chase the opposite sex, and the list goes on and on.

HABITS are cultivated and nurtured by you and no one else and can grow to overpower you.

If you need a HABIT (and apparently they begin with boredom) how about creating a constructive one, such as attending church, coaching a Little League team, or volunteering for a community project. Your HABITS can pull you up or pull you down. Notice I didn't even mention drugs, because that's too dumb to even mention. Sex and lust are determined by one's level of self-respect and respect for others, the more respect you have for others the less these two temptations disrupt your career.

F. FAMILY … having a spouse is an educational experience, and having children is a higher educational experience.

It is the highest of honors to be labeled a "family man" or "super mom," which comes from doing your work day after day and yet being able to be a mom or dad.

This accomplishment requires internal fortitude as well as discipline and drive.

To borrow a line from Jack Nicholson's movie As *Good As It Gets*, having a spouse makes you a better person. Having a spouse keeps one connected to reality and civilization.

For thirty-seven years the only real hobby I had was my wife and our two great kids. I loved every minute of it, and they kept my internal pilot light lit all the time to cause me to go out and do my best.

G. RECIPROCATE ....

I have a friend and business associate who always says, "If you help others get what they want, then you will get what you want."

I believe this to be totally true (it's pure logic): if you are involved in sales and the customer wants to take sales to a higher level or reach a new market, then help them go there. Make sure at least part of what you are selling is involved in the plan. In the end you'll have what you want, and your customer will have what they want.

H. VIEW ....

I have always said and have heard others say that the view is better from the top. I didn't say "was" better but "is" better. If you say "was," then you indicate that you have been to the top a time or two but haven't been there in a while. The goal is to get there and stay. If you have to leave, then get back as fast as you can.

I worked with a guy named Jim who always maintained that if you weren't the lead dog the view never changed. This perspective is quite comprehensive but does leave a couple of options: to be the lead dog means to be the top dog in Sales and Marketing, but a good leader also has the ability to be back in the pack and show others how to get ahead.

Bottom line: strive to be on top, and strive to be in front.

1. LEADS ... I've heard more than one good insurance person say that one should never purchase leads. I'm sure that there are leads for sale out there somewhere that could help a person make a bunch of money; I just haven't seen this list yet.

   Word of mouth is the best lead and reference. These are based on customer satisfaction, are free, and have substance. Many leads can come from just listening during a sales call; this can bring forth much information. The more calls you make the more leads you can potentially obtain.

   I've heard that there will be a 3 percent positive yield from a list of names purchased, and I believe you can get 3 percent from a page in the phone book.

J. RAPID RESPONSE …. If you get a lead, jump on it fast, because they can vanish very fast.

K. READ….

Read books, hopefully this one; read articles, read product literature, read whatever relates to your industry. The more you read the more well versed you are to answer questions, guide a client, and be able to seek out features, advantages, and benefits of a product.

L. TIME … not a mystery and not elusive, its value and quantity is known, and it is manageable. The unknown factor is the exact amount in our lifetime.

We know that we have twenty-four hours in a day, and the experts say that we are supposed to rest eight of these hours (I've pretty much missed that one so far). As you can see by my above comments, I place a high value on family, community, and church; therefore I can use about 7 hours on these projects and two meals.

So now we are down to a nine-hour workday to slay the dragons and bring home the bacon. Here is where it's really important to have at least a working idea of what you need to accomplish in the coming week. Setting important appointments and a structure for the week will bring forth results. You can use your management to gain the sales you desire. Plan your travel patterns to maximize your sales calls.

I'm known as a guy who never eats lunch. When on the road I can make three sales calls while others stop for lunch. This is not to say that taking a key customer out to lunch or an evening meal can't be quite rewarding. And there is nothing wrong with playing golf with a customer, but I can't ever document making a sale while playing golf. Fun is fun and work is work; which one pays the bills?

M. SALES TRAINING .... a modern-day tragedy

When was the last time you heard someone say that he or she was going to a SALES TRAINING session sponsored by his or her company? It is my observation that people in the business world feel that this is an unproductive and archaic activity. I think that I'm correct because of the level of salesmanship I encounter, the basic fundamentals just are not there.

I've lost count of the total number of these sessions I have attended, and I gained something from each one—if not from the instructor, from someone else in the session.

Sales training is not archaic; it's refreshing.

Thus we've nearly exhausted the alphabet and you've devoted a couple of valuable hours to reading this book.

I have shared some ideas and some of my past with you. It is our past and ideas which we use to build the future.

The future begins in about thirty seconds so lay down the book, look up, and see or envision your next Sales & Marketing opportunity..

www.ingramcontent.com/pod-product-compliance
Lightning Source LLC
Chambersburg PA
CBHW020253290526
45784CB00003B/1232